101 PROMISES TO HOLD ON TO

W. PATRICK HARRIS

Edited by
KAREENA GRACIA-DESIR

KW Syndicate Publishing

Copyright © 2022 by W. Patrick Harris

All rights reserved.

No part of this book may be reproduced in any form or by any electronic or mechanical means, including information storage and retrieval systems, without written permission from the author, except for the use of brief quotations in a book review.

Contents

Preface	vii
Introduction	ix
1. Rain Strengthens Flowers	1
2. Doggy Paddle	3
3. I Am Nibbles	5
4. Access Denied	7
5. Get Cooking	9
6. A Look at the Numbers	11
7. Spilled Beans	13
8. Your Future is Not Your Past	15
9. The Don't Worry Promise	17
10. Fine at 89	19
11. Joy	21
12. Through, To, and Away	23
13. Storms and Sunshine	25
14. Scratch Your Eyes Out	27
15. Strong Will, Strong Pill	29
16. These Rocks	32
17. Golden Brown	34
18. WHYYYYYYYY	36
19. Anything, Everything, Even As Thou Wilt	38
20. Strong-Armed	40
21. Spring Sprung	42
22. Timing is Everything	44
23. Extreme Makeover	46
24. For me, to me	48
25. Float on 2 overcome	50
26. No More Hope	52
27. Faith To Make It	54
28. Being Thank-Full	56
29. Everything Works	58
30. Never Forget	60
31. I Won My Case	62
32. Stay on Board	64

33. The Difference a Letter Makes	66
34. When Nothing Else Will Do	68
35. God of Goofs	70
36. The Birds	72
37. The Lion, Porcupine, and I	74
38. Double for the Wait	76
39. Flip Flop Don't Stop	78
40. The Turnaround	80
41. Fly	82
42. Rent	84
43. No Stopping	86
44. It Wasn't Pretty	88
45. Rise up	90
46. Of All Places	92
47. Unprecedented	94
48. Wait for Your 8	96
49. The Other Side	98
50. Wrestling Giants	100
51. Alternative Choice	102
52. The Answer Is	104
53. Less is More	106
54. Rattled or Focused	109
55. Eye on You	111
56. Just Call Me Faithful	113
57. The Recipe	115
58. Idle Angels	117
59. Creator Prepare	119
60. "THIS" "THE" "AN" "CAN" "WILL"	121
61. Believe is an Action Word	123
62. The Technique	125
63. Fear-Less	128
64. Go in Peace	130
65. The Little Things	132
66. There Will Be Days	134
67. The Handoff	137
68. Do the Math	139
69. Strengthening Therapy	141
70. Help/Hope	143
71. The Fixer	146
72. Seek Means Try	148
73. Who You Gonna Call?	150

74. Bring a Rope	152
75. My God is Greater	154
76. My "OH Reply" Is Coming	156
77. Break Every Chain	158
78. I Won't Complain	160
79. The Death of Death	162
80. Persistent	164
81. 5 Smooth Stones	166
82. Andre the Giant	168
83. Can You believe?	170
84. Detour to Destiny	172
85. Rest Stop	174
86. AUTO ON	177
87. Shanghaied	179
88. The Tearless	181
89. Time	183
90. Super Bloom	185
91. Troubled	187
92. Believe and Start Home	189
93. Current Condition	191
94. Fall In Place	193
95. Fear or Faith	195
96. CSI	197
97. Willing, Able and Ready	199
98. Supreme Package Deal	201
99. Victory Over Giants	203
100. It's Only Temporary	205
101. Sometimes you have to deal with the dogs	207
Afterword	211
Also by W. Patrick Harris	213

Preface

Welcome to the Hold On Family. To learn more about our outreach ministry, our other publications and our products that you can wear and share with others, simply go to:

Holdon2overcome.com

Introduction

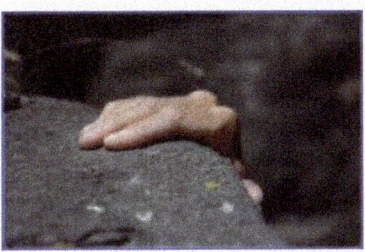

"Hanging in there" is a popular response to "how are you doing?" That term itself "hanging" leads to imagery and manifestations of struggles, helplessness, desperation, grief and even death. Hanging is by the neck until dead. Few people survive a hanging let alone experience a breakthrough or a victory from hanging. The startling realization for us today is that we don't have to hang because someone else hung for us. Therefore the message for everyone is that nobody has to "hang in there" but instead we can grasp on to promises and the power to fulfill them. So the response and the message then becomes Hold On! With your hands, feet, teeth by any means necessary. Though the rope may be burning and you're holding on to a thread just Hold On. All things will work out in time if you don't let go. It has happened for others and it will happen for me! How will I know if I let go? So, HOLD ON!

The ME is the personal part. These messages are meant for you reading this right now. In this book there will be occasions where you are invited to say your name and at that point you are welcoming a personal experience, acknowledging you are not alone and claiming the possibility of a breakthrough. You will also hear us refer to the Hold On Family. We are the people that have had to endure through the trials and tribulations, the situations that have tried to break us and all the sleepless nights. Now you are part of a family that will encourage each other to never give up or give in. We will not quit or stop trying. We are the determined, the motivated, the inspired. If God said it, we believe it and that settles it.

May the words on these pages speak life, love and hope to you and forever remind you that you are not alone.

Rain Strengthens Flowers

Babygirl is crying. She's just sad. Daddy has promised that his lap and his arms will always be a place of solace and so he sits and holds her, whispering a prayer and rubbing her back. He looks out the door and onto the deck where he sees this pot of flowers being pelted by the raindrops that are falling and pretty heavily at times. The petals are so delicate and fragile. They bob up and down with the impact of each raindrop, left then right maybe trying to avoid the next drop but to no avail. Your heart almost goes out to these brave, struggling little flowers until you realize that's how they grow. They need the rain to make them stronger.

Daddy says, "Baby girl, look at the flowers. After the rain ends they will stand up taller and be even more beautiful than they were before." Family, we are flowers and in our lives some rain must fall. Matthew 5:45 tells us "so that you may be children of your Father in heaven. He causes his sun to rise on the evil and the good and sends rain on the righteous and the unrighteous." Isn't that a wonderful reminder for us today that trouble doesn't last always? These words are an encouragement, a source of peace and a promise of hope. Just remember that the rain clouds will pass and the sun will shine and then we too will stand taller, stronger and be more beautiful than before.

"*Lord, thank you for the rain. Please help us, comfort us and keep us through these storms like You said you would. We ask that you again just speak the word peace over our lives. In Jesus' name we claim it, Amen.*"

The forecast is *sunny*. We just have to Hold On.

HoldOn 2 Overcome. H2O

Doggy Paddle

This is a true story. A family is out boating and they take the family dog onboard for the ride. They get back to shore and discover the dog is missing so guess he must have fallen overboard and after a diligent search they give the dog up for lost. The next day the dog miraculously just shows up at their campground where they were staying. They calculated that he must have swam three miles back to shore and then walked another six miles to actually find the family. This is a true story. A family is out boating and they take the family dog onboard for the ride. They get back to shore and discover the dog is missing. They figure he had fallen overboard and after a diligent search they give the dog up as lost. The next day the dog miraculously shows up at their campground where they were staying. They calculated that he must have swam three miles back to shore and then walked another six miles to actually find the family. But Hold On a minute, if he was 3 miles offshore he probably couldn't even see land so how did he know which way to swim? What dog can swim three miles nonstop and after he got to shore how did he know which way to walk? Do you think he got tired along the way, *dog tired* perhaps or was that dog focused on one and only one thing - reuniting with his family? Did he just keep imagining the reunion and how happy they were going to be to see him again? He had to know how much the family loved him and how great it was going to be to have them hug and rub him to pieces. The bowl of food that would be offered. The crisp, cool water in his own bowl. His own bed, his yard, his tree, the abundant treats... surely he was talking to himself the whole way, "Just keep paddling....keep walking... keep going. *Hold On and you will see your family again.*"

Was it a miracle? Surely it was but it was also a lesson in faith exemplified by a dog. Faith *is* the miracle. When all seems lost you point yourself in the direction of home and paddle. Don't stop paddling or praying. There may be more than one challenge so don't be discouraged if after all the paddling you may still have to walk to reach the destination. Remember, He promised a reward for your labor if you just keep going. (Jeremiah 31:16) Let's claim it and speak the affirmation right now. [*Say your first and last name*] today is a great day to reach your destination. Today, is a great day, for my breakthrough.

TODAY, IT'S P2O. PADDLEON 2 OVERCOME.

I Am Nibbles

This is Ms. Nibbles, the escape artist. Don't let that little face fool you. She is a few ounces of hurricane. She has jumped, dove and ran away more than a few times. It's so bad that I'm the only one that will even attempt to remove her from her cage. Once she was lost in the house for 3 days. So it is really nothing short of a miracle that she is sitting here in my hand rather calmly to take this shot. You see I was determined to tame her and change some of her natural tendencies to better help her fulfill her purpose of bringing joy to our home. Ms. Nibbles wasn't fulfilling her destiny so I came up with the idea to put her in the sink. The surface is glazed and the sides are so smooth and high that no matter how hard she scrambles those little paws she can't make it to the top and out. Oh she tries. She will run and run like on a treadmill but can only get up so far. Then she learned to use it like a half-pipe and launch herself from one side to the other and did get over the edge once only to land in the trash can below. So the trick was to put her in the sink and wait until she got completely worn out and weary of scrambling for the edge. Then I sat my hand in the sink offering her a place of solace and after a few weeks of this "training" she would climb onto my hand, sit there and even allow me to pet her. Hallelujah! Then it hit me. *I am Nibbles.*

Second Kings 19:28 and Isiah 37:29 both say, "Because you rage against me and because your insolence has reached my ears, I will put my hook in your nose and my bit in your mouth and I will make you return by the way you came." Hold On Family, just consider for a moment that our bowl experiences just may be God's way of trying to save us to help us fulfill our destiny. Sometimes some of us require as the Bible termed it a "hook and bit" to teach us and maybe we will have to "return by the way we came" before He can take us forward. Whatever the case, we all have a purpose. I don't know about you but I'm ready Lord to sit safely in your hand. Proverbs 3:5,6 says "Trust in the LORD with all your heart and lean not on your own understanding. In all your ways submit to him and he will make your paths straight." I [*say your name*] am Nibbles and if Ms. Nibbles can learn to rest in someone else's hand, then I can learn to rest in God's. How about you today? Are you ready for your destiny? Then pray it and Hold On because today, is a great day, for that breakthrough.

HoldOn 2 Overcome. H2O

Access Denied

I've been going to lots of funerals recently. I bet you don't have to think very long before remembering a time when your very life was in danger. Maybe you were so tired that you fell asleep driving at the wheel? What about that truck or car that swerved and barely missed your car or that time your car spun around several times and just came to a stop in the middle of the road. Ever experience chest pains or a night you just couldn't stay asleep? Hold On Family, know and believe that our enemy the devil is a roaming lion and he has a funeral planned for each and every one of us. Daily he tries to shake us, weaken us, separate us from our protection and strength. He is relentless in his attempts to claim our lives when we are at our worst, but God!

Job 2:6 "And the Lord said unto Satan, Behold, he is in thine hand; but save his life." Yes, it is a fact that there is a battle waged every day, hour and second for our very lives and just like He did with Job, God through grace and mercy says *"No. Access Denied. You can not touch this life!"* Many times you can literally feel it. There's just something working behind the scenes. In that moment when your life passed before your eyes, when you knew you were no longer in control and felt helpless to save yourself. Those times when things happen so fast that you don't even have time to process it or even pray. Hold On

Family, if you are reading this today I propose that God has intervened and saved your life more times than you could ever count. More than trillions of times. If He saved your life it's for a reason. So Hold On. God is not finished with you yet! There are two great days in every person's life. The day they are born and the day they find out why. Always remember that you are special and valuable. You have a purpose and you are still here under the guidance and protection of your Heavenly Father as He prepares you for your destiny.

So HoldOn 2 Overcome. H2O

Get Cooking

*T*he pressure is on. In Esther 4:16 it is recorded that Esther has agreed to fast for 3 days and then in Chapter 5:1 it states "On the third day Esther put on her royal robes and stood in the inner court of the palace, in front of the king's hall." As we read it is quite clear that Esther went before the king on the third day of her fast and in verse 4 made a request. "If it pleases the king," replied Esther, "let the king, together with Haman, come today to a banquet I have prepared for him." Hold On Family, did you catch that? On day 3, before she went to the King to ask him to come to dinner Esther had already done the cooking. Esther went to the King prepared for the desired outcome. What boldness, what confidence, what assurance. Before entering the court she even said "If I perish, I perish." Wow, what a proclamation of faith to fill us with hope today.

With only a few days and death looming ahead she is acting in faith. Esther is *cooking*. While the others are still fasting and worrying, I imagine they are also probably wondering where the queen is and what she is doing? Esther is wearing an apron, boiling, peeling, chopping and marinating. She's preparing a whole banquet feast fit for a king. There is a song that comes to mind. "Don't wait till the battle is over to shout now. You know in the end, you're going to Win!" Don't you give up, give in, or despair. Instead, heat the oven and cook. God said it, I believe it and so that makes me the chef.

Today is a great day, to enjoy the feast.

So HoldOn 2 Overcome. H2O

A Look at the Numbers

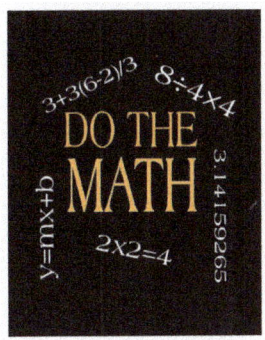

Let's consider time broken down into numbers. We all know that one day is equivalent to 24 hours but did you realize that 24 hours is actually 1440 minutes or that 1440 minutes is comprised of 86,400 seconds. Then 86,400 seconds are actually 86, 400,000 milliseconds spread out over time. Hold On Family, we've come a long way since yesterday. Today at this very moment and with each passing second we are even closer to the breakthrough than we've ever been before. Every tick of the clock brings us closer to that blessing, that harvest, the fulfillment of dreams and promises.

Closer to the healing. Closer to freedom. Closer to the revelation. Closer to completion. Closer to the reunion. Closer to the end of the battle, the struggle, the attack. Closer to… the close. So be joyous and shout today because the celebration is closer than it's ever been before.

Jeremiah 1:16 says "there will be a reward for your labor." So whether you look at it as 1 day or 86,400,000 milliseconds, Praise God because you are still here and victory is SURE. The enemy can't stop time from passing and every single millisecond of it brings us closer to his defeat and our victory. So pray, believe and Hold On. Since you started reading this now you're already approximately one minute or 60,000 milliseconds closer to that breakthrough. You can make it. You will make it. It's only a matter of time.

JUST H2O. HOLDON 2 OVERCOME.

Spilled Beans

The children were dressed, packed and ready for school. I was completing their lunches and in my haste I dropped a bowl of hot baked beans. In slow motion I watched the bowl slip and I knew "this is going to be a BIG mess." Sure enough the bowl hit the floor with a grenade effect casting warm, sticky beans on everything and in all directions. Time stopped for a few seconds as we just stood there with our mouths open surveying the damage. In that moment the thoughts came in succession. *1. Thank God we have more beans 2. Praying for those that would gladly eat these spilled beans even off of this floor 3. This is my fault, how could I do something so stupid? 4. I can't leave it like this or it will be an even worse mess later. I have to clean it up now. 5. We're probably going to be late for school.*

Hold On Family, have you ever "spilled the beans?" Do you have a sticky situation that you're trying to deal with? Do you think or feel you've made a mess of your life? Well picture this. Jesus is standing there looking at you. He's wearing an apron and a pair of those yellow rubber gloves while holding a bucket of steaming-hot, soapy water in one hand and a brush in the other with a big towel thrown over his shoulder. You have to wonder where did He come from and how did He know about this so fast? How does He know about all the messes I make? Then He speaks, "Just stay there, I'll come to you." He drops the supplies, opens His arms wide and then just hugs you tightly to His bosom rocking back and forth a little and speaks softly in your ear, "Don't worry, it's going to be alright. I'm here now and I won't leave you." Then Jesus, while still holding you sings softly in your ear, "Jesus loves the little children. All the children of the world...." Suddenly a chair appears and Jesus gently seats you in it then steps behind you to start massaging your shoulders. He lightly jokes about the mess and assures you that "this is really nothing at all." Then you notice that the mess is disappearing as you talk with Him. He stands you back up, renewed, refreshed and clean. He winks and casually says "It's what I do child. It's what I do." Revelation 3:20 "Behold, I stand at the door and knock...." Ready to clean. That's what He told me to tell you today. Stop worrying, over-thinking, hesitating, procrastinating and guilt-tripping. Just give Him the mess and Hold On. It's what He does child. It's what He does.

JUST HOLD ON. HOLDON 2 OVERCOME. H2O

Your Future is Not Your Past

Sliding into bed last night my daughter, "Babygirl" asked, "Daddy, can you read the Bible to me?" Picking up the Bible I answered, "Of course, what would you like me to read?" She said "Something with a long chapter." Immediately my mind centers on the book of Isaiah and I start flipping to that book and settled on a page. I asked her to just pick a number and she replied 9. I felt a tingle of excitement as I looked down and realized that my page-turning had landed me right at Isaiah chapter 9. "Ok Lord, that is no accident so what do you have for us here?" Isaiah 9:1 "Nevertheless, there will be no more gloom for those who were in distress." Wow! Translation: In the future there won't be any more suffering from what has plagued us in the past. Translation: I hear your prayers [*say your name*] and I'm going to end this chapter of your struggling and give you peace and joy.

Hold On Family, you're going to make it. He knows the plans He has for your future. The problems of your past will not follow you into your future. That brothers and sisters is hope and a promise because God said "will be." Claim the promise right now and make it personal, "I will be clean and sober. I will meet the right person. I will be a graduate. I will be employed. I will be disease free. I will be financially stable. I will be…

saved." So Hold On, Hold On, Hold On. Tomorrow is your future and that's a great day, for your miracle.

So HoldOn 2 Overcome. H2O

The Don't Worry Promise

Don't worry. Sometimes it can even be annoying for someone to tell you that. It's like they are dismissing the seriousness of your situation. Sounds easy enough for small things but on larger issues like your future, love, family, even matters of life and death how can you expect someone to just not worry? No one has yet to give me any concrete methodology on how to not worry. So I'll share what I'm learning on my own journey.

Don't worry means letting go of it or maybe another way to put it is not trying to be in control of it. Whatever it is. Then you realize "I am not alone so I don't have to deal with it alone." To take it even further I decided to help solve the problem for the entire world by developing a tool to help any and everyone not worry. I'm almost finished with my new invention. It's a pair of glasses that you put on as soon as you feel yourself about to begin to worry. Looking through the glasses they project a picture, an image in front of you of... Jesus.

You can choose what your own Jesus looks like. He's your personal Jesus that you know and have a personal relationship with. With the glasses on you will see this Jesus standing there with His arms open wide. He's saying "Just look at me, focus on me and let it go. I have this and everything else too. I AM with you and I AM in control. I'll work it all out for your good." So whenever you have the glasses on, whatever you look at you have to look "through" Jesus to see it. I call them "D.W.E.T. Don't Worry Eyewear Trainers." Trainers because you won't always need them. Your own "Don't Worry Vision" will get better, stronger and finally be completely corrected. Guess what? Everyone can afford them because I'm giving them away free of charge. No bills or payment plans to worry about. I only ask for a prayer in return.

Matthew 6:25-34 and Luke 12:22-31 both say *don't worry* and those words are God's own words that we can read, claim and repeat back to Him as His very own promises that *can not fail!* Hold On to your new glasses but don't worry. If you lose them you can easily get another pair and at no cost. Just pray with me and Hold On.

HoldOn 2 Overcome. H2O

Fine at 89

A little math. Sarai, Abram's wife, is actually 10 years younger than he is. We know this because it is recorded in Genesis. 17:1 that Abram was 99 years old and then in 17:16-17 God tells Abraham that his wife Sarai will have a child. She will become the mother of nations and her name will be changed to Sarah. Abraham asks "will I have a child at 100 and Sarah at 90?" Conclusively, Sarah is 10 years younger than Abraham. Now back to Genesis 12:4 where it states clearly that Abraham is 75. So when he took Sarah into Egypt to escape the famine Sarah was 65 years old. Yet she was so attractive that she gained the attention of everyone that saw her (verse 14), including the Pharaoh himself. Abraham tried to say she was his sister thinking they may kill him to get to her.

Hold On y'all, Sarah is so gorgeous that they can't even cover it up. The men who are usually scouting the kingdom for young, attractive, virginal women rush to the palace to tell Pharaoh there is a new beauty in town and she's a shop-stopper. Imagine Pharaoh with anticipation coming in to later discover that they have brought him this old woman. That scout would get the axe, literally. No, you didn't play games like that with Pharaoh. So Sarai really had to be fine at 65. Now remember in chapter 17 Abraham is 99, so Sarah is 89. In Chapter 20 Abraham moves his family to live in an area called Gerar. Again Abraham is afraid for his safety due to the beauty of his wife (what a problem to have, right?) so again he plans to call her his sister. Then the local King Abimelech sees her and is so smitten that he takes Sarah away to be his own. The Word says took. But wait a minute, does this King realize that he is running off with an 89 year old woman? That's a great grandmother, and quite possibly she's older even than King Abimelech. Why? Apparently Abimelech hasn't learned to ask the crucial questions while speed-dating. Eighty-nine, been married for decades and *still* this woman is runway worthy. Imagine Abimelech finally finding out that he got hooked by the same woman that beguiled the Pharaoh more than two decades ago?

Hold On family, here's the realization and cause for praise that we can apply to our lives, loves and situations today. "If God promised it, it will come to pass." God told Sarah back in Chapter 17 and she even laughed at the news in Chapter 18 that you will have a son. And if my God said it, it will come to pass! He *will* keep you, sustain you and preserve you so that what He said, will come to pass! A baby at 90? YES. Do you need healing, a job, a home, food and water? Maybe you are asking for weight loss, the right mate, freedom from addictions or incarceration? We could go on and on but the fact is anything you can possibly think of, the answer is still yes! Genesis 21:1 "For Sarah conceived, and bare Abraham a son in his old age, at the set time of which God had spoken to him." Yes, Sarah was still *fine at 89,* preserved by a promise and kept for a purpose. So today I'm going to do my part with what I put into my mouth and my mind. I'm going to exercise and claim God's promises. But even beyond these things we all have a purpose and if you think it hasn't been fulfilled yet in your life, Hold On. If God promised, it *will* come to pass. Won't you claim it with me? Not just physical beauty but life everlasting. There are no time limits with God.

So keep Holding On and we will Overcome.

Joy

*J*oy? Did it really say joy? James 1:2 "Consider it pure joy, my brothers and sisters, whenever you face trials of many kinds." Sometimes, to get an understanding of His Word we just have to have a conversation with God. "Lord, how can I possibly think that this, my life, my situation, my problem, is joy? Apparently you do not understand the depth of this situation. Don't you see me here in this mess? I'm broke and broken. This is anything but joy. You just keep saying wait. What did you say God? Keep reading, there's more."

James 1:3 says that "because you know that the testing of your faith produces perseverance." Wait a minute God. Did it say produces? Does that mean something is going to come out of all this? This isn't the end? It won't always be like this? What was that God? Remember what? Joseph didn't *stay* in the pit or the prison. Noah didn't *stay* in the ark. David didn't *stay* a lowly shepherd. Paul didn't *stay* in prison. Moses didn't *stay* in the wilderness. The Israelites didn't *stay* in slavery. Jonah didn't *stay* in the whale and Naaman didn't *stay* a leper. And Jesus didn't *stay* in the tomb." Hold On Family, did you notice that there's a pattern here? The trials eventually produced, led to, ushered in a breakthrough and yes, joy.

"God, so you're telling me that just like you did with these people in the Bible you're using the trials to produce the victory in my life? The Trials Produce Victory? T.P.V. OK God, I can see it now and if you will stay with me, right beside me and let me feel your presence I believe that I too can have the victory and the joy."

That's what this message is all about Hold On Family. We are here today to tell you that there can and will be joy. You are here today to receive and believe this message and then pass it on to someone else that needs to be reminded also. Yes, joy. Joy comes in the morning. Just Hold On for it.

HoldOn 2 Overcome. H2O

Through, To and Away

In Exodus 14:7-9 the fleeing Israelites fear for their lives as every single horse, chariot and soldier in all of the Egyptian army thunders towards them with bad intentions. Moses stands up to say, "Fear ye not, stand still and see the salvation of the Lord, which he will shew to you today: for the Egyptians whom ye have seen today, ye shall see them no more again forever." These recently liberated slaves had witnessed quite a few miracles in the recent days and so they aren't beyond believing in possibilities but the difference is that each of those miracles left traces or debris. There were mounds of dead stinky frogs and all the vegetation that had been lush and green was bare after the hail and the locusts. There were sores and scabs after the boils. Every miracle had left evidence of its occurrence but now Moses is saying that they won't see any more of these oppressive Egyptians, period. Forever.

Sometimes we just have to believe and Hold On especially at the predictions of the seemingly impossible. God has a purpose and a plan for these children of His. God is about to take them through, to and away. *Through* the water (baptism by immersion) and then bring them to a new place fulfilling His promises. For the climax he is going to wipe *away* all evidence of their past lives as fearful slaves. Verse 14 says "The Lord shall fight for you and you shall hold your peace. Now read verse 28, "And the waters returned and covered the chariots and the horsemen and all the host of Pharaoh that came into the sea after them; there remained not so much as one of them."

For whoever is reading this right now, God is reminding you that He promised and He will take you *out* of the bondage of mistakes, lessons, trials and tribulations and *into* the promise/fulfillment/breakthrough. For good measure He will even clean up the mess that would have been left behind. You don't have to take the old bondage or baggage with you. The waters covered the Egyptian army completely and the current of the river carried them all downstream and away to be gone forever. The Israelites could go on to their new home in peace and confidence knowing they would not be pursued or even reminded of the old life that they had left behind. One moment they were scared to death, traumatized and facing the impossible and then minutes later they stood there watching the water flow by calm and serene with no sign of a threat. Are you tired of seeing it, fearing it, fighting with it? Let's pray.

"*Dear Lord, thank you for your promises to me. Now I ask today that you bring me through, bring me to and wash it away and you will get all my praise. In the name of Jesus I claim it, Amen.*"

He promised through, to and away. Today, is a great day, to see that miracle.

JUST HOLD ON. HOLDON 2 OVERCOME. H2O

Storms and Sunshine

Yesterday a serious thunderstorm just blew in. Sun one moment, thunder and lightning the next. I went to a window and looked out to realize that just over there, maybe a quarter mile away, the sun was still shining. There was a marked line where the storm clouds ended and the blue skies began. Strange perhaps? I say not at all. Why? Well, I say "My God." But let me clarify that I'm not referring to some general mother nature/power in the universe theory. No, there's no credit going to atheistic explanations or spiritual ideologies. The scientific professionals could take a stab at explaining with their meteorological models and diagrams but nope, that's not it either. So why was it storming over here and sunny over there?

Matthew 5:45 says "That ye may be the children of your Father which is in heaven: for he maketh his sun to rise on the evil and on the good and sendeth rain on the just and on the unjust." Hold On Family, right then, somewhere, there was somebody praying for rain. At the same time there was somebody else just right over there praying for sunshine. The God I'm trying to serve, the one in heaven that we pray to… He can do anything and both at the same time. His Word says, "The wind and the rain, they obey thy will." So it's no surprise that there are clouds here and sun right there because when there is a storm here, there is still the *Son* up there above it and the Son shines through and around the clouds. Hold On and pray through the trials. Hold On and keep believing. Hold On and stop worrying. Hold On and know that our God can do it because today, is a great day, for the *Son* to break right through my clouds.

JUST HOLDON 2 OVERCOME. H2O

Scratch Your Eyes Out

True Story. I was maybe a teenager and my mother announced that some family friends were stopping by our house for a visit. The Arthur family arrived: dad, four daughters and a young son. The young people were all standing in our driveway talking when all of a sudden one of the girls started screaming hysterically. Then, one by one the other girls joined the first one screaming, crying and running around in circles covering their eyes with their hands. They were so terrified and of what I had no idea. They clamored, scratched and clawed their way up onto the hood and then roof of their dad's car. For the gold medal award for weirdness, they were all sitting there shaking and crying, covering their eyes with both hands. It really was a strange scene. I mean I've spent quite a bit of time in our driveway and there has been a snake or two, a neighbor's dog, even a fox but no such terrifying beast was present now. What on earth could make supposedly sane people put on such a show? Then it appeared. Strolling from under the car emerged this horrible beast seemingly laughing. A whole whopping five pounds of ....cat! Yep, they were all so deathly afraid of just a cat that they believed would scratch their eyes out!" (Hence the eye covering) Ok, sounds ridiculous right?

If it seems silly to fear and worry about things that are so comparatively small and harmless, then why am I [*say your name*] so worried about my small problems with such a big God? Just repeat this now, "Father, I give it all to you. You are in control. You are in control." Now release it. Raise your hands, bow your head and give some thanks. Uncover your eyes, get down off that car, compose yourself and have a great day. Stop worrying, God is in control.

"*Lord, I pray that whoever reads this message today will feel your presence, your power and your peace over their lives. We believe that You are greater than all our problems no matter how big or how small. Lord, You are strong and mighty, the King of Glory, mighty in battle, the Prince of Peace, Amen.*" Now Hold On because today, is a great day, to stop worrying about it.

HOLDON 2 OVERCOME. H2O

Strong Will, Strong Pill

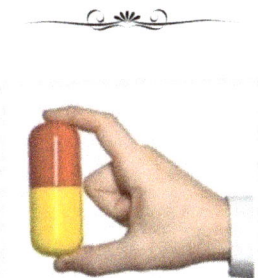

*E*very human being at one time or another will ask the question why? Why this? Why that? Why ME? And if we are honest we will admit that we usually ask why when something unpleasant happens. We don't question the good stuff that happens to us? Who would find a $100 bill and ask why is this happening to me? We innately believe that we should have positive experiences. We like to believe that we deserve blessings and favor, breakthroughs and harvests. We all love being winners but losers not so much. Even within the church the concept of prosperity means you are doing something right and God is allowing you to reap all the good that you naturally deserve. Truth be told some of us struggle with having to struggle. It's sometimes hard to believe that there is a loving and caring God when we suffer with so many problems.

Imagine this. We have all contracted this fatal virus called sin and we are suffering from the symptoms. God, the great physician specializing in sin recovery is prescribing a treatment plan to save our lives. The recovery rate is remarkable but the process can be a challenge, uncomfortable, even painful at times. The results are sure for everyone *if* we stick with it and some people just may take a little stronger prescription to cure what ails them. Some of us may need a more aggressive medication. Some of us seem determined to die so God will have to bend us right to the point of breaking in order to save us from ourselves. The bigger and stronger the *will*, the bigger and stronger the *pill*. In other words there is a loving and caring God and He does see you in your situation but He has looked into your future and He knows that He will have to to allow the pain, the problems and the trials in order to save you. (Help ME Jesus) He can see the road ahead and the outcome of the path you are on at any given moment. He has looked forward into time and like a chess computer He has calculated every possible move and then developed a strategy with the best chance of beating this disease and getting you to glory. You were strong-willed, set in your ways, dare I say hard-headed and on a path to destruction so God had to incorporate some unorthodox tactics and non-traditional strategies to get your attention. In order to beat the virus He had to convict your mind and convert your heart. Jesus went all the way "out-of-the-box" just for you. Then He took the wood from the box, made it into a cross and allowed them to hang Him on it, just to save you.

Ezekiel 18:26-32 If a righteous person turns from doing right and commits sins, they will die for it; because of the sins they will die. But if a wicked person turns away from the wickedness and does what is right, they will save their life. Because they have considered all that they have done wrong and turned away from them, that person will surely live and not die. Yet some people say, "The way of the Lord is not fair." My children, are my ways unfair? Isn't it really your ways that are unfair. Therefore children, I will judge each of you according to your own ways, declares the Sovereign Lord. Repent! Turn away from all of your wrongdoing; then sin won't be your downfall. Rid yourselves of all the wrongdoing you have committed and get a new heart and a new spirit. Why should you die my children? I don't take any pleasure in seeing you suffer or die declares the Sovereign Lord. Repent and **LIVE!**"

The message is strong wills will usually require strong pills. God is a loving, caring attentive parent that has done everything

He could possibly do to save us. Jesus is offering the cure and it's paid for in full. Maybe it had to be a visit to a hospital to get your attention? Maybe some people are going to have to live broke and busted because God knows money would destroy them. Some people are hurting right now because of a broken relationship not realizing God was sparing them future misery. Hold On, these uncomfortable situations just may be the pill God uses for your breakthrough. Keep pressing and never stop praying because today, is a great day, for the cure.

HoldOn 2 Overcome. H2O

These Rocks

I try to do my complaining on my knees and although we don't want to seem ungrateful or unfaithful sometimes we have to pour it all out to someone that really can make a difference. God tells us in His Word that He cares for us and He invites us to cast our cares on Him. So it was on one of those days during an avalanche of problems that I found myself thinking out loud.

These rocks, God these rocks. Can't you do something about all these rocks that just keep coming? Every time I turn around, no matter how hard I try, pray, or obey, these rocks just keep rolling down on me. Day and night, night and day from every direction. My shoes are scuffed and my toes are bruised and bleeding from kicking these rocks on my path. I even got hit in the head by one the other day and I thought it was going to kill me. Then God answers, "Well child, remember that I told you it could be like this. Don't forget that you're living in a construction zone and there may be some rocks and debris here and there. It may not be pretty and it may get a little dirty but I'm doing something great in your life right now. We've come too far to turn back now so don't give up. Just Hold On, I'm moving that mountain out of your way."

So whoever is reading this right now know that if you are

also encountering rocks it's only because you too are in your construction zone. God is blasting and hammering away at that mountain to show you how it's done. 1 Corinthians 13:2 and Matthew 17:20 both tell us that faith does move mountains so just repeat this, "The rocks are evidence that He's moving my mountain. He's moving my mountain!" Now give a shout of praise and Hold On. Keep going and keep praying. Today, is a great day, for that mountain to be gone!

Now HoldOn 2 Overcome. H2O

Golden Brown

*A*dmittedly, I love sweets. No alcohol or drugs for me but a sweet roll, a warm-out-the-oven cookie or a hot slice of apple pie with sea-salt and caramel vanilla ice cream... hmmm. I digress. My mother taught me to bake from scratch. I can still recollect mixing bowls, sweet aromas and the memories of licking spoons. If you spent any time in the kitchen then you learned that to get the desired result of that perfect pie or cake there is this process that actually sounds quite harsh. The directions say to "Crack/break" some eggs. "Whip" some cream. "Mix" the batter. "Slice" the apples. "Grate" the cinnamon. "Crumble" the chocolate. "Stir" the liquid. "Shake" the pan. "Crush" the breadcrumbs. "Sift" the flour. "Squeeze" the lemons. "Spread" the icing. "Melt" the butter. "Pound, Roll and Knead the dough." Fire up" the oven and then leave it in the extreme heat for a long period of time awaiting the sound of the timer indicating that it is finished. It rises and bakes and then at the precise right moment it will be removed from the heat to fulfill its delicious purpose.

JOB 23:10 "BUT HE KNOWETH THE WAY THAT I TAKE: WHEN HE HATH tried me, *I shall come forth as gold.*" Hold On Family, just like that pastry we are going to *"come forth."* Forth from the beating, the pounding and then forth from the heat just like that pastry, golden, warm and wonderful. My Father is taking all these ingredients and using a recipe designed just for me to produce something marvelous and wonderful and it's going to be sweet. The Word says "Taste and see that the Lord is good" and we are going to taste it. Just Hold On for it because today, is a great day, for the timer to go off and I [*say your name*] will come out of the oven, golden brown.

Now HoldOn 2 Overcome. H2O

WHYYYYYYY?

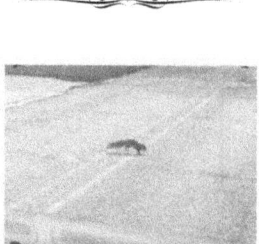

$\mathcal{D}$eer are renowned for it but today it was a squirrel. I saw it sitting right at the side of the road and it waited, waited right until the moment I was just close enough and then it ran right across the street in front of my car. It disappeared somewhere under the vehicle and I couldn't even tell if the spinning wheels had ended its furry little existence. Why? Why wait until the car is right there? Why play with your life like that? There are always flat squirrels by the roadside. Hold On a minute. Do we ever act like squirrels? Ask yourself, "Am I [*say your name*] running between the car tires?" Only you can really answer that question but if there is something that you know needs to change in your life. If you have tried and failed, if every day is a day of vowing that this is the last day and the last time, if something has to give, I invite you to give these words a try:

"*Father God, thank you for all you've done. There are things that I cannot do and so I ask you to please help me, change me, save me. In the name of Jesus, Amen.*"

The Word says "all things are possible" and "I can do all things." Know that you are not powerless and that you are not alone. The thing you are struggling with will not control you. You *can* beat it. Today is the first day of the rest of your life and a great day for the miracle of *change!*

. . .

HOLD ON FOR IT. HOLDON 2 OVERCOME.

***H2O Family, This message is especially for the brothers and sisters battling addictions. Whether we can admit it or not, we are all struggling with something so there is no judging or condemnation, only HOPE. Please feel free to reach and send a message to us. You can also get support by calling or going to the Substance Abuse and Mental Health Services Administration website or call 1-800-662-HELP.

https://www.samhsa.gov/find-help/national-helpline

Anything, Everything, Even As Thou Wilt

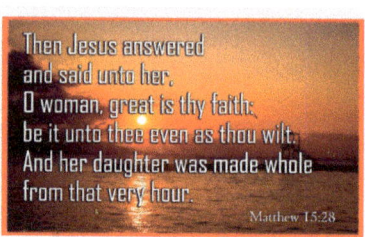

Then Jesus answered and said unto her, O woman, great is thy faith: be it unto thee even as thou wilt. And her daughter was made whole from that very hour.
Matthew 15:28

*I*f words have meaning.... and the words of our prayers have power.... then is it reasonable that the power of our prayers are strengthened or weakened by the words of our prayers? Listen and examine your prayers then ask what would happen if God answered my prayer *literally* as spoken? Just as I prayed it?" Hold On a moment and think about that. For example, how many people pray to be cured of a disease and then have the same sickness come back? God answered the prayer but now you're battling the same thing again. Why? In Matthew 15:22 the Syrophenician woman came to Jesus with a problem. Verse 25 reads "Then Jesus answered and said unto her, O woman, great is thy faith: be it unto thee *even as thou wilt* and her daughter was made whole from that very hour."

Hold On Family, if we're going to pray to a God that says He can do *anything*, why not ask Him to do *everything*. "Lord, please heal me and never allow this sickness to return." That day Jesus made that woman's daughter completely whole, never to suffer from those demons again. Momma went home and found a daughter cured of all sickness and diseases, even smiling with a pleasant attitude. Now she gets up on time and makes her bed, comes the first time she's called, does her homework, doesn't talk back and loves modesty. Hallelujah, she is completely healed and forevermore.

"LORD, WE NEED YOU TO FIX IT LIKE ONLY YOU CAN. THE ENEMY IS powerless and you are all powerful. So today we claim it in the name of Jesus to make us whole never again to see or deal with this problem we are bringing to you now and we will give you all the praise, honor and glory, Amen."

FAMILY, HE ANSWERED THAT MOTHER'S PRAYER SAYING "EVEN AS thou wilt," meaning as you asked. Let's go to that same God with the same determination and faith today. Know that today, is a great day, for a complete answer to my prayer.

JUST HOLD ON FOR IT. HOLDON 2 OVERCOME. H2O

Strong-Armed

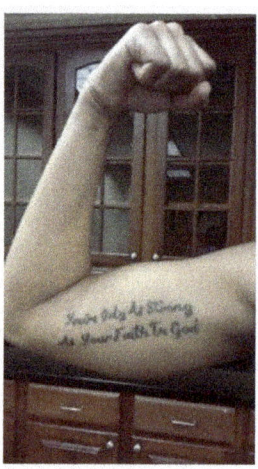

I was greeted by the smile of a stunning young woman at the front desk. When she raised her arm I noticed this tattoo. I enquired and she responded "I have a story." I thought for a moment about how tragic a story could such a young person have? We often compare our journeys to those of others and sometimes consider their needs and feelings less serious than our own. As I left that office I just couldn't forget this young woman and the look in her eyes. So I turned back around, went back to that office and asked her point blank, "What is your story?" Maybe she just needed to talk. How often does God send us to help, to comfort, or maybe just to listen and talk she did. I stood there listening and had to take several deep breaths as I shook my head at what she revealed. She gave a chronological exposé and emphasized each stage in the saga with "there's more... and then.... that's not all." The story just kept going, deeper and more intense. Tears could not be contained. There is a young woman attached to that arm and be assured there are thousands of young women and men just like her. They are God's children and no matter the circumstances He loves them, sees them, hears their hearts and will answer their calls.

See, it's not just our story or past, our trials, tribulations or failure. It's our faith and willingness to allow God to heal and restore us. You can believe in your own strength and rely on the pick yourself up methods if you'd like but just be prepared to keep falling down. That arm will forever declare that "You're only as strong as your Faith in God." I know you too have a story and it is not finished yet. Hebrews 12:2 says "looking unto Jesus the author and finisher of our faith..." And Isaiah 66:9 reminds us, "Would I bring you to the point of birth and not deliver?" God lifts, restores and finishes what He started. Say it out loud. "God is not finished with me [say your name] yet." Have faith and keep holding on for it because today, is a great day, to declare your victory.

So HoldOn 2 Overcome. H2O.

Spring Sprung

Well, did you hear Him? Did you get a sign, see a miracle, find a clue? Has God spoken to you recently? Take a moment and think back over the last few days and remember what caught your attention. For me it was seeing these little budding flowers on the ground. In that same spot there was snow just one day ago and there were no flowers there earlier in the day when I walked by to leave. So sometime today, in just a few hours they received the signal and sprang forth. I just noticed them there when I came back and could not help but think that these flowers were a definite signal that spring has arrived.

Hold On Family, those fragile little flowers are declaring a big powerful message. All it takes is one day for that miracle to spring forth. Just like these flowers you can get up one morning covered in dirt and later that afternoon be basking in the sunshine. Song of Solomon 2:11-12 says "For lo, the winter is past, the rain is over and gone; The flowers appear on the earth; the time of the singing of birds is come and the voice of the turtle is heard in our land." Those little lavender flowers are a sign and a reminder to us today that all it takes is a little time with Jesus and that's why I'll Hold On.

I'll Hold On for that one special day when my snow will melt and my flowers will bloom and today, is a great day, for my breakthrough. Today, is a great day, for your breakthrough. So get ready to shout "Spring has sprung, thank you Jesus."

HOLD ON [SAY YOUR NAME]. JUST HOLDON 2 OVERCOME. H2O

Timing is Everything

     I'm driving down the road having it out with God. Twelve rounds of spiritual battle for the championship. I'm battered, bloody and my eyes are nearly swollen shut from the beating I've been taking but like Jacob I'm determined to "not let go until you bless me." I have come too far and endured too much to give up now. So I'm driving and arguing out loud with God and I don't even care who's watching. Sometimes you just have to do that. Just talk and pray it out loud.

    Don't be afraid to challenge God, He can handle it. Matter of fact that's what we need Him to do. Please handle it Lord. Right then at that very moment next to me this big black truck merges into the lane to my right and...BAM! There is a big white cross painted on the back tailgate. Then there was this message painted underneath the cross which read "KEEP ON TRUST'IN." Under that were the words "GOD IS IN CHARGE." What could I say but "thank you Lord for the message. Your timing is perfect. You must have heard my cries. You are in charge and I'll Hold On."

    Hold On Family, I'm going to challenge you today to step into the ring and go a few rounds with God. Then get ready for it, anticipate it, start looking for His answer. Be aware and on the lookout for billboards, license plates, bumper stickers, even bird formations. Answer every phone call that comes and go to the mailbox expecting miracles. Listen intently to conversations and that radio/tv stations you just happen to be surfing by. Watch that sermon that someone sent you the link to because Jeremiah 33:3 says, "Call unto me and I will answer thee and shew thee great and mighty things, which thou knowest not." How will you know it's Jesus answering because He was the only one that knew your question. His timing is perfect. His timing is everything. Today, is a great day, for Him to be right on time.

SO, HOLD ON. HOLDON 2 OVERCOME. H2O

Extreme Makeover

*J*ust a couple of months ago these new apartment buildings were filled with residents. Then one day there were fleets of moving vans moving everybody out. Shortly after that the construction crews arrived. They removed the vinyl siding (exterior covering) and I thought they were just redecorating. Then they removed the Tyvek (water/moisture barrier). Then the windows and the plywood, all the interior drywall and insulation, all the way down to the steel skeleton of the building. This was no simple redecorating. Upon inquiring I learned that there was a mold infestation so everything had to go. This was going to require an Extreme Makeover.

Yes, it reminded me of me. And if you think about if for a moment you might get where this is going. I [*say your name*] am experiencing an extreme makeover. Redecorating the surface isn't going to be enough this time. God has to completely remove, reshape and repurpose me to what I could and will be if I allow Him to. Genesis 12:2. "I will make you into a great nation and I will bless you; I will make your name great and you will be a blessing." That's a promise from God Himself, with 4 "wills" all the way back from Genesis. He has always offered blessings for those that choose Him and not just for personal prosperity because the last "will" is for us to be a blessing. That's the purpose, to be a blessing. Do you want to be a blessing? If you do say it with me, *"Lord, I want to be a blessing."* But let's be honest, the demolition is not easy and it will be uncomfortable. We just may have to cry out, "But God, it hurts." Then He lovingly replies, "I know but Hold On child. I'm going to make you.... beautiful." So be encouraged and focus on the finished product. You are in the hands of a renovation expert and today, is a great day, for Him to reveal the finished product.

JUST HOLD ON. HOLDON 2 OVERCOME. H2O

For me, to me

*A*CV. Apple Cider Vinegar. It's good for you but if you've ever tasted it you would probably agree that it's not necessarily so good to you. But if we think about it for a moment very few things are both good to you and for you. If it tastes good, like a whole chocolate cake, it might be good to you but not so good for you. That consistent exercise program, it is surely good for you but it's gonna hurt sometimes. Today we spend most of our time and efforts trying to find a healthy balance between what's good *for* us and what's good *to* us. I hate the job but need the money. I love to shop but need to save. Everything is a compromise and we often try to rationalize away our actions or inactions while trying to find a happy medium.

Maybe that's why we don't exercise our faith. We've gotten so used to not having it all that we just don't think it is even possible so not worth pursuing. Is there anything that can be good *to* you and *for* you? Well I propose that there is. God is. He is good to you and good for you, because He is God *to* you and God *for you*. His name is Jesus and He says in Jeremiah 32:27 "Behold, I am the Lord, the God of all flesh; is there anything too hard for Me?" Hold On family, He is there when we need to go *to*

Him and He is there working it all out *for* our good. There's no either/or with Him who is all things to all people. No compromising with the name above all names. Not A.C.V., but G.O.D. So we can be encouraged today with the words of Romans 8:31 "What, then shall we say in response to these things? If God is for us, who can be against us?" Just trust Him today and don't let go. *"Lord, give me strength for what you're doing to me and Lord, I trust you to work it all out for me. Amen."*

This is not the time for giving up. Today, is a great day, for that breakthrough to arrive.

HoldOn 2 Overcome! H2O

Float On 2 Overcome

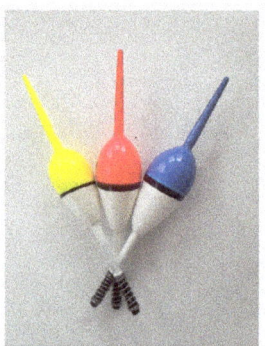

If you've ever gone fishing you'll recognize that little gadget as a float and floats, just like people, come in all different sizes, colors and kinds. Round, square, short, long. There are floats for streams and floats for the ocean depending on what kind of fishing you may be doing. The remarkable thing, the miraculous thing, the thing most admirable about a float is... you can't hold one down. You can't drown a float. Push it down and it pops right back up. Hold it under and it reaches for the sky. Over and over and over again. Hold a float down and it never stops pushing, stretching, ever striving... upward and it seems almost happy doing it. There is a lot to learn from a float. So how about we adopt a float mentality and just never stop trying. Let's pray.

"Father God, thank you for letting me see another day. I come today as your child to claim every promise in your word about restoration, reviving, rising and your returning. No matter what the circumstances, Lord help me today to float. In the name of Jesus I pray, Amen."

I think I'm going to put a little float in my pocket as a

reminder that you can't keep a child of God down. He promised me in Jeremiah 31:16 that there will be a reward for my labor and today, is a great day, for me to break through to my miracle. Float On [*say your name*].

FLOATON 2 OVERCOME. F2O.

No More Hope

Can you imagine living with no hope? Well, you do realize that when Jesus comes there will be no more hope. Let me explain. From the first day of kindergarten through the twenty two plus years it takes to become a surgeon, a student *hopes* their way through each step. Hoping for grades, hoping for finances, hoping for the final graduation day.

While you are a student, you look forward to finishing and the day when you won't have to be a student any longer. We all hope for that day. But at graduation, on graduation day… You see it now? 1 Corinthians 15:52 "In a moment, in the twinkling of an eye, at the last trump: for the trumpet shall sound and the dead shall be raised incorruptible and we shall be changed." Just think about it. At the appearance of that cloud the size of a man's hand. When the angels burst through the clouds and at that trumpet sound there will be no more hoping for change, because the time has arrived when we will be changed. No more awaiting arrival, because arrival has arrived.

We will never have to hope again because everything we could possibly have hoped for is supplied. Therefore, no more need for hoping. No more hoping for healing because you're healed. No waiting, no wondering, no questioning, no theorizing, no delays. All your family, all your friends, all your dreams, all your wants, all your desires and Jesus. Hold On for the day when not having hope will be a good thing. Hold On for the day when we will get to leave our earthly hope behind and then live forever with our heavenly hope, Jesus. Today, is a great day, to put your trust in Him.

HoldOn 2 overcome. H2O.

Faith To Make It

Five years. That's a long time to be unemployed. But that was what she said, "I haven't had a job in 5 years." Now just take a few moments and imagine what it would be like if you hadn't had a paycheck for 5 years. What happens after the unemployment and the benefits run out? After the COBRA period expires and you've borrowed from everyone that would listen. You have a home, children, utilities, etc.. After all the interviews, headhunters, temp assignments and insulting offers. Hundreds of them but no permanent jobs or paychecks. Even after there has been much prayer and fasting, imagine no income for five years.

But Hold On Family, she also reported that she was never evicted, never hungry, never without necessities. The bills somehow got paid. Each month, every month, month after month something came through. Miracles, blessings, true friends, temp jobs, bill reductions, loan forgiveness. It's a process but over time you learn to... lean on Him. Talk to Him. Rely on Him. After giving it your best and your all and after you've done all you can..., you just stand, (or kneel) open your arms wide, hold your head back to heaven and whisper "I can't, you can, I give it all to you Lord." Fact is, if you've never been there you're probably going to have to go there to really learn the lesson on letting go of self and leaning on the Lord.

No matter what you read, hear, think, or believe you can't save yourself or there wouldn't be something called drowning. God can't save you either if you are in the way thinking and acting like it's you who are in control. Read John 14 today where Jesus Himself says "I am the way, the truth and the life." Who saves the drowning, keeps roofs over heads and food on tables for 5 years with no job? Jesus. You better recognize and Hold On to Him. We all will have to learn to let go of self and Hold On to Him for life itself. And after a while you start expecting the miracles you couldn't even see before and that's when we discover real faith. We're going to need faith to make it through those days, weeks, months and yes maybe even years.

FAITH TO HOLD ON. HOLDON 2 OVERCOME. H2O

Being Thank-Full

More snow means more shoveling. For senior citizens inclement weather can be a nervous time. They can worry about things like getting to the store, getting their mail, even going to the doctor if need be. So on these snowy days I prioritize my shoveling efforts according to age and ability. First I dig out the 90's, then the 80's, working my way down to the 70's and 60's. Years old that is. For the 4th out 5th time this winter I knocked on Mrs. Willet''s door to let her know it's me and I was here to help. I started clearing her porch methodically working my way down the steps to the driveway. She opens the door with a big smile that says she's more than happy to get her snow removed. The snow is simply a good reason to enjoy the good company and our warm conversations. OK I confess, I look forward to it. She is just a joy to be around.

While I'm digging in the snow she says, "I would give anything to be able to do that."

I pause for just a second to look up. Why would anyone want to shovel snow? Then I let it all sink in. She's standing there between the arms of her walker for stability, her hair completely white now. Glasses hanging around her neck next to her emergency call button. She speaks through the glass because the cold is colder when you're 90 years older. She adds "I used to love to shovel snow."

I turn back to the shoveling and put a little more back into it full of thanks that I can still shovel snow. I can walk and see and drive, hear, dress myself and hug my children. I realize there are a lot of people that just can't do some of those things any more. Colossians 3:15 says "And let the peace of God rule in your hearts, to which also ye are called in one body; and be ye full of thanks." Hold On Family, no matter what transpires today, I [*say your name*] can still find something to be full of thanks for. As a matter of fact I can find a lot to be thank-full for. If I'm reading this right now, Hallelujah that means I can see. I'm conscious, educated and better off than many less fortunate all over this world. Yes, I am blessed and today is a great day, to be *full* of thankfulness.

HOLD ON. HOLDON 2 OVERCOME. H2O.

Everything Works

Have you ever needed transportation or had your transportation break down? When you couldn't afford to fix it or maybe it's just on its last leg and not worth fixing? Imagine not being able to get to work, carry groceries or pick up your children from school then driving by dealerships and seeing hundreds, even thousands of new cars just sitting there unused. Over time your desires evolve from a new car with a specific color, make and model to "give me anything Lord, that works." It may even seem strange to pray for a car when there are people praying for food or shelter. But if you need a car you need a car and God knows it. If you've been there then you may also know the feeling of being so thankful and relieved to be the new owner of an old "hooptie." You can be ecstatic about a clunker you never would have even considered before. You're just happy you're not standing outside anymore and although it's not the newest model with the newest features, everything works. May not be the desired color or brand but it's cold outside and the heat works in this old bomb. Raining, but the wipers work. All the windows may not work but all the doors open and you got it with no money down and no credit check.

Philippians 4:19 "But my God shall supply all your needs

according to his riches in glory by Christ Jesus." Hold On and know today that "Our Father is rich, in houses and land. He holds the whole world in the palm of His hands." That includes cars. It also covers test results, relationships, businesses, tuition and anything else you may need. He has it *all* in His hands. You just need to Hold On. It may come in a form you hadn't considered or expected. Keep praying and know that when God provides it, everything will work just fine. EVERYTHING. Today, is a great day, for a working miracle.

JUST HOLDON 2 OVERCOME. H2O

Never Forget

I had been reminded of something I forgot and was speaking to a group of kids about it. I told them that I forget a lot of things and a little boy just spoke out in a comforting way. "Everybody forgets things." I was still shaking my head at the realization that I/we often get so busy running to and fro that things just slip our minds. How many things get misplaced and lost in the sauce. The wallet, the keys and the cell phone just to name a few that go missing on the regular for me. Sometimes we feel that as adults we should be held to a higher standard. I asked "are you sure, everybody?" The world stood still for a small instant as that little boy thought and then smiled up at me and said "everybody but God." If ever there was a mic drop moment that was it.

Hold On Family, that was wisdom from the mouth of babes. From the mouth of God himself He reminds us in Deut 4:31 "For the LORD thy God is a merciful God; he will not forsake thee, neither destroy thee, *nor forget* the covenant of thy fathers which he sware unto them." And again in Isiah 49:15 "Can a woman forget her suckling child, that she should not have compassion on the son of her womb? Yea, they may forget, *yet I will not forget thee.*" As a matter of fact the entire Word of God is a reminder and a promise to us that God will not forget us. If you forget everything else today, remember this. First, God is God. Secondly, He is not dead. Third, He has not forgotten me. Fourth, He is on the throne working for my good and fifth we have to Hold On, Hold On, Hold On. Today, is a great day, for that miracle. Never forget, He never forgot.

Now HoldOn 2 Overcome. H2O.

I Won My Case

Those were the words that breathed LIFE into me. A friend called me and right on time. "Remember my problems with my previous employer," she asked? In that moment I thought back through some of the details of how she had been falsely accused, singled out, mistreated, slandered, abandoned by friends and finally wrongfully terminated from her job. Have you ever been talked about? Been the subject of gossip? Had your very character questioned and had down-right lies spread using your name? Sometimes it seems that the enemy will prevail in his attempts to drag you through the mud. Living a life of shame can be overwhelming. Especially when the crowd has been blinded and seems to align against the truth. These are the times that we discover who our true friends are. Well this woman was experiencing all of that and now she is reporting that God answers prayers. After the evidence was considered, the testimonies given and the deliberations were made, God *fixed it!*

After two years of struggling, mentally, physically, financially and spiritually, the truth was brought to light, the accusers were silenced, justice was served and she was vindicated. "I won my case!" she shouted. We had to stop right there on the phone and have a praise break session.

Psalms 119:31 says it well. "I have stuck unto thy testimonies:

O LORD, put me not to shame." Hold On Family, we are going to stick to God's testimonies of His Word. Hold On and we will repeat Psalms 44:7 which says, "But thou hast saved us from our enemies and hast put them to shame that hated us." Hold On and claim the promise of Isaiah 61:7 "For your shame ye shall have double; and for confusion they shall rejoice in their portion: therefore in their land they shall possess the double: Everlasting joy shall be unto them." Hold On Family, it's not over yet." No weapon formed against me shall prosper, it won't work." No matter how dark it may seem, justice *will* prevail. Why you ask? He's a doctor in the sickroom and a judge in the courtroom. He sits high and looks low and He promised that His children will always come out on top. We are going to win this case called life. Just Hold On and be encouraged today.

HoldOn 2 Overcome. H2O.

Stay on Board

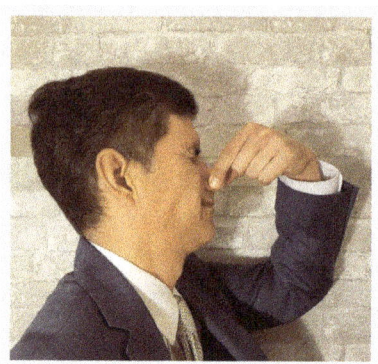

We were sitting in the sanctuary for an afternoon presentation by a profoundly deep man that had everyone's undivided attention. On the pew in front of me sat the "A" family: father, mother, young daughter and young son who was playing quietly. All of a sudden, "Brrraaaam-mmppppp!" Young son unabashedly let's one go loud enough to be heard by anyone within a couple of pews. The parent's heads snap in horrified awe at the prospect that it was one of their own progeny that had so unashamedly "cut the cheese" in church. As they looked my way I opened my eyes wide and chuckled, "It wasn't me." Yes, it was a moment to go down in history and also a powerful lesson because the boy never stopped doing what it was he was doing. He didn't get up or leave. While others were gesturing and being embarrassed he kept right on playing like nothing had even happened. So Hold On Family, why do so many of us, the adults, decide to leave the fellowship of God's house/church when something happens, doesn't go our way, or makes us feel uncomfortable?

Mark 4:38 "And there arose a great storm of wind and the

waves beat into the ship, so that it was now full. And he was in the hinder part of the ship, asleep on a pillow: and they awaken him and say unto him, Master, carest thou not that we perish?" The message today by a little boy's flatulence and 2000 years ago by Jesus's disciples is no matter what happens, stay in the boat! Through storms, discomforts, pain, embarrassments, stay in the boat. Why? Because Jesus is in the boat with you. Verse 39 "And he arose and rebuked the wind and said unto the sea, Peace, be still. And the wind ceased and there was a great calm." Though the boat may rock, Hold On to the sides. Though troubles may come, Hold On to the saints who will pray with you. Hold On to His promises and the storm will be silenced.

Yes the church is full of messy and messed up people. Consider the church a hospital for sick people to receive treatment and we all are dealing with one ailment or another. But that's where the healing is and it's not from the people, the pastor, the choir, nor the leaders, it's from the universe-renowned surgeon and CEO, Jesus. Yes, people are going to break wind in church and it just may be you sometimes. But beyond going to church to receive a blessing God expects us to go to church to *be* a blessing as well. We, every single one of us, are on the medical team and have a part to play in the healing of the nations. So remember that little boy and the smile on his face because today, is a great day, to come back home.

HOLDON 2 OVERCOME. H2O.

The Difference A Letter Makes

*T*ake a look at these two words, literally. The spelling. It appears that these two words in the English language are very similar with a lot in common. They are synonymous and interchangeable. Imagine replacing the word Wait with the word Faith to get, "I'm FAITHING on the breakthrough." By swapping the words Hebrews 11:1 could be translated into "WAIT is the substance of things hoped for, the evidence of things unseen." The word wait by definition as a noun that means "a period of waiting." But the definition as a verb means "to stay where one is or delay action until a particular time or until something else happens." Doesn't that sound like faith which is defined as "a strong belief, complete trust, confidence?" Now combine these two definitions together and we can read: "Having a strong belief, complete trust and confidence for the period of time before/until something happens." Lord have mercy. I couldn't make that up myself.

That Family is the definition of faith and the Hold On motto. Oh, it's going to happen just like He said it would if we just Hold On. Acts 27:25 reminds us that if God promised it, it's just a matter of time. We just have to put our Faith into action during the time until it does. That's the waiting part. Psalms 27:14 says "**wait/faith** on the LORD: be of good courage and he shall strengthen thine heart: **wait/faith**, I say on the LORD." Whoever you are reading this right now, you are not alone and your prayers are getting through. It won't always be like this and whether you are waiting, faithing or a combination of both today, is a great day, for that miracle.

HoldOn 2 Overcome. H2O

When Nothing Else Will Do

*A*t different times our priorities and desires change. There are times when we would like new shoes and other times when we really need new shoes. Times when we could use help and times when we have to have help. Times when we hope for a break and times we are praying that we don't break. There will be times when it is sink or swim, live or die. Actually, some of us may be at a time right now when nothing else will do but a miracle. (Help us Jesus) When you've stopped counting single dollars because you need thousands. When you have done your best and exhausted every potential resource. When the date isn't approaching because the deadline is here. There is no paycheck coming because you're unemployed. You've had the curative surgery, a breast or a limb removed but now the cancer is back and the doctors have had that "nothing more we can do" talk. The enemy's plan did work and I am defeated. Yeah, those times.

So I have a question for those who don't believe in the Lord and Savior Jesus Christ. If we all have those above mentioned kinds of moments and days, what do you do? See, we here at H2O we believe. We have had enough of those experiences to have to believe and not just what we read in some book or saw on the internet. These sorts of times are beyond what you will learn at a meditative enlightenment conference. These are the life or death moments that grab us in the midnight hour, the help me Jesus experiences. We here at H2O believe because we have witnessed enough first hand life altering miracles in the lives of others. We believe that there was a group of people facing a flowing river ahead and with an approaching army behind. There was a group of people surrounded by the enemy and so hungry they would eat anything. There was a man lowered to lions and some boys marched to a fiery furnace. So today I can Hold On because I *know* that when nothing else will do but a miracle, I can expect one.

"Father God, thank you. Now today in the mighty name of Jesus I claim that the same power and promises from your Word be manifested in my life. Now grant me peace and assurance that it is done. For your glory, Amen."

WHEN NOTHING ELSE WILL DO, HOLD ON.

God of Goofs

In this picture Tanner the dog is experiencing and expressing guilt. Ordinarily Tanner is energetic and friendly with just enough aggression to be protective toward his family but today Tanner has goofed up. Right now guilt has changed the way Tanner looks and acts. The great Tanner is reduced to this timid, whining, seemingly dejected and defeated mutt. We actually feel sorry for these poor animals caught right in the middle of their mess but does his owner banish him, punish him, or stop loving him? Does God banish us, punish us, or stop loving us? NO. Someone said those words to me the other day and it sure hit home. "God is a God of Goofs." Wow! Admittedly, I am a goof and if you are honest you can admit it too. I'm a mess and I messed up but we don't have to hang our heads with guilt. Just like Tanner is no less a dog or member of his family for his infractions (although he did have to spend some time outside the house for his actions), God assures us in Hebrews 4:16 "Let us therefore come boldly unto the throne of grace, that we may obtain mercy and find grace to help in time of need."

Hold On Family, just come. Anyway, anyhow and in spite of the mess just come. You can apologize for all your goofs and ask forgiveness. Determine not to let it happen again and try your best. The first step is to just come. Don't let the enemy press you down with the weight of guilt. Look up and see Christ's arms open wide and hear him saying to you, "No matter what, I still love you and nothing you do will change that. I told you in Romans 8 that nothing can separate you from me child. "Neither death nor life, angels nor demons, fears nor worries, not even the power of hell. No power in the sky above or the earth below, indeed nothing in all creation will ever be able to separate you from my love." Thank you Jesus for that message and for loving us. Even us *goofs*.

HOLD ON. HOLDON 2 OVERCOME. H2O.

The Birds

Notice anything about these two pictures. I was sitting by a window and looked out to see the scene in these pictures. Through the pouring rain it looked at first like statues sitting atop the roof until one moved a little. I realized that it wasn't statues but birds hunkering down in the storm. Birds, all lined up there, heads down to their chest with their wings covering their bodies. Then as the rain slowed and eventually stopped I was able to get the lower picture. The birds were still sitting there in the same exact place. They began to lift their heads and spread their wings. Then they began flapping their wings and shaking off the water. Now that the storm was over it was quite evident that they were actually drying their wings out, preparing to *fly*.

Hold On Family, what a lesson for us today. During the storm we can rest our heads on our chests and fold our wings in that same position. Well actually since we don't have wings yet we can fold our hands and pray. In just a while the rains will end and we too will raise our heads and raise our hands to shake off the remainder of the storm and prepare again to *fly*. The word tells us that we can look to nature for lessons and as this scene unfolded before me I was amazed by the testimony and the action of these birds. I want to remind you today of Matthew 6 which says, "Behold the fowls of the air: for they sow not, neither do they reap, nor gather into barns; yet your heavenly Father feedeth them. Are ye not much better than they?" Hold On and remember these birds today. Unworried, unshaken, unwavering and undefeated. "His eye is on the sparrow and I know He watches ME." Pray and wait out the storm. Then head up, hands outstretched and dry your wings. Today, is a great day, to FLY!

Hold On. HoldOn 2 Overcome. H2O.

The Lion, Porcupine and I

We were standing there peering through the glass at these animals. Although they are no longer alive they are still exquisite examples of what they probably looked like before the trip to the taxidermist. I was just staring and talking out loud when I added "... but they weren't created like that. The big teeth, the long, sharp claws. Even the porcupine didn't have those long sharp quills."

My friend looked at me inquisitively wondering how I would know these facts so then I added "It's because they didn't need them. At creation there was no killing, fighting, ripping, or tearing. The porcupine had no reason to need defense mechanisms, because there was no need for defense. Actually, they were all vegetarians and got along in perfect harmony.

Genesis 1:29,30 says "...everything that has the breath of life in it, I give every green plant for food." Guess what? They will be like that again one day soon. There's hope for us today in a world gone mad. Storms one after the other. Wars, many at the same time. While obesity is killing some folks, others are starving to death. Corporate CEOs making billions while company employees are going hungry. People abusing the very ones they were supposed to love. What was up is down and right is left. And that's why I can have faith, in faith. Because there just has to be more for mankind than this earthly existence with all its tumultuous turmoils. God please, just help it make sense.

His Word explains it like this: Mankind has a past and a future. In the past He created everything good and perfect including man. Man was given the chance to live forever in peace, *if* he chose to but man made a choice that affected the DNA for all mankind, passing on the negative effects of the first man's bad choices. God has a plan for the future to fix and restore man's past mistakes and forever correct the DNA so man will never again need crutches, alarms, drugs, lawnmowers, glasses, or guns. If you just had to eat flesh down here on earth then you might not want to go to heaven because nothing will die any more and there won't be any 3-legged cows or one-legged chickens.

We all can believe and take comfort in knowing that the peace and perfection that was in the beginning will exist again. God has promised and He is going to fix it. He will restore this earth to it's original and intended beauty. This promise isn't just for us. Genesis records that there were many creatures created on land, in the air and in the waters. God made the lion, the porcupine and *me*.

So Hold On for that great day when we will be rid of all the weapons and defense mechanisms because we won't need them anymore. No doctors or pain, no crutches or canes. No funerals or glasses, no traffic or angry masses. No predators or prey, joy and happiness all day and talks with Jesus by the sea of glass. All we have to do is Hold On.

HOLDON 2 OVERCOME. H2O

Double for the Wait

I was speaking with a mother about parenting. She had decided to be a stay-at-home caretaker and I was encouraging her in the fact that her job really is the most important job on earth. Her children have become models of success and the subject of great admiration. The mom then shared the real story and confided that she and her husband had been trying to have children for the first 10 years of their marriage. There were no physical problems and all medical evaluations were positive. They are part of a culture where children are a big deal on both sides of their families. The husband was one of 12 children and the wife was one of six children both in Latino families so producing offspring was more than a big deal for them.

They decided against fertility drugs and so for ten years they tried and prayed. Then one day one of those "little swimmers" turned on the last lap of the relay race and with a burst of super strength crossed the finish line for the win. But to the joy and amazement of the crowd the replay sonogram image revealed that it was actually a tie. The news travelled quickly through both sides of the family. TWINS!

Genesis 18:14 says "Is any thing too hard for the Lord? At the time appointed I will return unto thee... and Sarah shall have a son." Chapter 21:1,2 says "the LORD visited Sarah *as He had said* and the Lord did unto Sarah *as he had spoken*. For Sarah conceived and bare Abraham a son in his old age, *at the set time* of which God had spoken to him." Isn't that an encouraging message especially for those of us that have been waiting and waiting? The Lord did, "As He had said...As He had spoken...at the set time." Now take a moment and ask yourself, "what specifically did the Lord say He would do for me?" What promise can I stand on? OK, say it. Repeat it. Write it down and claim it! (I'm preaching to myself now). Don't worry about how long you've been praying or waiting, just know and believe that He blesses *Double For the Wait*. If He said He will, then He will, at the set time. Habakkuk 2:3 "For the revelation awaits an appointed time. It speaks of the end and will not prove false. Though it linger wait for it. It will certainly come and will not delay."

Every time I see those twin girls or any twins for that matter I am forever reminded to Hold On. It may linger but it certainly will come and if you think twins are really something special, just wait till you see a set of triplets or quadruplets. Hold On, because today, is a great day, to receive *Double* for the wait.

HoldOn 2 Overcome. H2O

While this message serves to be inspirational we want you to know that we lift up special prayers for families, marriages and relationships. We remember those that may be facing challenges starting their family and those coping with the over-abundance of multiple births. We are continually praying for blessings on families.

Flip Flop Don't Stop

I caught this little guy in the picture at the riverside with a plastic bowl. (To prove to the kiddos I could do it.) I picked him up and placed him in my hands so we could get a better look at him. What a lesson in life this little swimmer is. He had no arms to try to break free. No legs to press my fingers apart or run. All he could do was *flip flop* back and forth. And breathe. His little mouth opened and closed in coordination with the gills doing the same. To all appearances his situation looked bleak. Some creature a thousand times his size has grabbed him up and has taken him captive. But you know what captured my attention and amazement. This little guy is a fighter. HE WON'T GIVE UP! He just keeps flip flopping back and forth all over the place (trying) and breathing (praying) as his little body heaved in and out. He would give it *all* he had, then rest for a moment. Give it his all again, then rest for another moment. Then start the process all over again. But even during the apparent moment of rest, He still kept breathing (praying).

That's our message for today from a baby fish. Flip-flop but don't stop. If you need to just repeat those words to yourself throughout your day then try it. *Flip flop* just don't stop! If you come across someone that needs it share the story and the word with them. We *flip* and we *flop* but we won't stop! Also don't forget to breathe (pray). We walked back to the water's edge and gently set that little fish free to go on his way again, surely not knowing the impact he had had on our day. If that little fish can keep going, so can I. *Flip flop*, don't stop until we overcome.

HoldOn 2 Overcome H2O.

The Turnaround

*E*xodus 14. Here we are just after rejoicing about our recent deliverance from one problem when we find ourselves again under attack from the enemy. We've followed God's directions and kept on the path as He directed but still we are standing with the deep sea in front of us and an attacking army of soldiers closing in back of us. The sea in front is impossible/impassable and the army behind is impossible/impassable. We might as well accept our fate because there is just no way out. We are doomed. Then suddenly the sea opens in front of us and everyone walks through the water on dry land to the other side. Just as suddenly the sea closes again, conquering and covering the enemy that was chasing us.

The same water that just a little while ago had been the problem, the impossibility, the barrier, has now become at God's design and command the solution. Hold On family, God can turn your situation completely around. He can make barriers into blessings, burdens into benefits and bitterness into breakthroughs!

They were afraid of the water, challenged by the water, depressed because of the water. Then rescued through...the water. And this wasn't the first time for Moses. Remember that as a baby the same river that was meant to drown him, carried him in that little basket to Pharaoh's daughter. God did it then and He can do it again right now for you and I. Exodus 14:4 "And I will harden Pharaoh's heart, that he shall follow after them; and I will be honored upon Pharaoh and upon all his host; that the Egyptians may know that I am the Lord. And they did so." That very thing you are worried the most about? Pray the prayer of turnaround. Your greatest challenge can become the turnaround. The wayward child, turnaround. Unemployed and bills are due, turnaround. The loneliness and failed relationships, turnaround.

Let's pray. *"Father, thank you for all you've done. Now please take my burdens, my barriers and my bitterness and turn them into my blessings, benefits and breakthroughs. I will let the world know you did it and give you all the praise and glory. AMEN."*

Hold On, because He *can* do it. Today, is a great day, for your turnaround.

JUST HOLD ON. HOLDON 2 OVERCOME. H20

Fly

This little bird is only a few weeks old. I first took pictures as mom built the nest. She voiced her discomfort and anger each time I got anywhere near although she was living under my deck rent free. She would almost attack me. Then risking an aerial assault I took more pics when the eggs arrived and again when I noticed there were little baby birds moving in the nest. Their eyes were closed then but now, only a few days later their eyes are open and they are out of the nest and here. How did he get here? The nest is nearly six feet above and over there. He can't stay here. It's far too dangerous with all the hungry cats lurking around, like satan that roaming lion. Look at him. He can barely even hold his legs straight. Yet he is out of the nest and trying to fly with momma-bird. Momma is flapping and screeching down instructions from above and in spite of all the obstacles, baby bird is trying to fly.

 I read a quote earlier this week that is one of the best ever. "Father, what if I fall? Child, what if you FLY?" Just let that sink in for a moment. Here we are supposed believers and followers with the ability to actually talk with God right in His mighty presence, ...yet we are worrying and wondering. Nervous and anxious about what might happen if we let go and trust Him. Fearing the enemy's attacks over the Father's promises. Afraid to let go and let God. Hold On family, the Father knows what you are capable of. He made you and knows what you can and will do because... he knows what He will do for you. His promise in Isaiah 40:31 says, "But they that wait upon the Lord shall renew their strength; they shall mount up with wings as eagles; they shall run and not be weary; and they shall walk and not faint." Hold On, those are promises from God himself. Four shalls in the same verse and it says you will "mount up with wings" which means you will *fly*. Eyes on Jesus, believe and keep flapping those wings. Above the problems, attacks, setbacks and struggles. Hold On because today, really is a good day, to take off and *Flyyy*!

HoldOn 2 Overcome. H2O

Rent

The Bible records at least four places of residence for Joseph. At home in His father's house Joseph was well cared for. He had his own room, security, good food, even a custom tailored wardrobe but all of that changed. Subsequently he resided in some difficult situations. In Genesis 37:23-24 he is in the pit. "So when Joseph came to his brothers, they stripped him of his robe—the ornate robe he was wearing— and they took him and threw him into the *pit*." Then in Genesis 39:2 he resides in Potiphar's House. "The Lord was with Joseph so that he prospered and he lived in the *house* of his Egyptian master." But if we continue reading to Genesis 39:20 Joseph is now in a prison cell. "Joseph's master took him and put him in *prison*." Joseph finally makes it to the Palace in Genesis 41:40, "You shall be in charge of my *palace* and all my people are to submit to your orders." Hold On Family, I noticed something. From the pit to the palace Joseph never had to worry about or pay any… RENT! Psalms 91:11 "For he shall give his angels charge over thee, to keep thee in all thy ways." In Luke 4:10 we are reminded again, "For it is written, He shall give his angels charge over thee, to keep thee."

That's a promise from the Old and New Testament. While

He's preparing you for greatness, during the formative years, on the way to the palace, He WILL keep you. Psalms 37:25 says "I have been young and now am old; yet have I not seen the righteous forsaken, nor his seed begging bread." He told me to tell you today "Don't worry, I have you. I provided for Elijah, Moses, Joseph and a slew of others and I will provide for you [*say your name*] too." Now head up, chest out and don't worry about the rent. He has, is and will continue to *keep* you. Just Hold On.

HOLDON 2 OVERCOME. H2O

No Stopping

Enemy, be advised. I am not going to stop! If God sees fit to wake me in the morning and I have a breath in my body then I'm pushing on. I'm going to be busy today encouraging people. I'm going to take time to pray with people. If someone is down I'm going to lift them up. If someone needs an ear I'm going to listen. If I run into someone that says they don't know a savior, I'm going to share my story. If someone needs and I have it to give, I'm going to share. If God decides to bless me with a few bucks I'm going to be faithful and return His portion. If something or someone rubs me wrong I'm going to hold my tongue then loose it to pray for them instead. If someone is hungry I'll feed them. Enemy, you can try and I know you will but know that I am determined and you are defeated. No matter what and at all costs I will keep on going in the name of Jesus. You've tried but you can't go any further than my Father allows you to. I may shed some tears but I'm ok with that because victory will be mine. So enemy, you might as well stop right now because I won't stop! I will not give up, give in or let go. I will press on, Hold On and then Hold On some more because I know that I [*say your name*] will have a breakthrough today.

Psalms 121:1-8 "I will lift up mine eyes unto the hills, from whence cometh my help. My help cometh from the Lord, which made heaven and earth. He will not suffer thy foot to be moved: he that keepeth thee will not slumber. Behold, he that keepeth Israel shall neither slumber nor sleep. The Lord is thy keeper: the Lord is thy shade upon thy right hand. The sun shall not smite thee by day, nor the moon by night. The Lord shall preserve thee from all evil: he shall preserve thy soul. The Lord shall preserve thy going out and thy coming in from this time forth and even for evermore." That's a promise for us from our Father so be encouraged. Today, is a great day, to not stop. Instead let's Hold On.

HoldOn 2 overcome. H2O.

It Wasn't Pretty

It was an important game and I remember that we were down by 17 points with only two innings to go. The other team was relaxed, laughing and joking, already celebrating the victory considering they were ahead due to our errors, mishaps and self-implosion. It's our turn at bat and we happen to score three runs that inning but still it's too little too late as the inning ended with our team still way behind. We have one more chance and in that final inning on our last at bat our team rallies with bats on fire. Miraculously our last runner crossed home plate making the tally for our team 18 and sealing our victory. The next day when people asked how the game went I remember replying, "It wasn't pretty, but we won."

Read Deuteronomy 30:11-20 "Now what I am commanding you today is not too difficult for you or beyond your reach." Hold On Family, no matter what the score is in your life, it is not over yet! Nothing is impossible for Jesus Christ and He says in these verses that it is a choice, so *choose life*. Win or lose, live or die. Pick up your bat, walk up to that plate and swing claiming the promise for life. Declare with me today, "It may not be pretty, but I [*say your name*] will win." Then verse 20 says, "...listen to his voice and hold fast to him. For the Lord is your life..." There is the assurance in the Word that you *will* win, if you Hold On. Today, is a great day, for a game winning rally with your name on it. Pretty or not, you win! That's all that matters, you win!

Just Hold On. HoldOn 2 Overcome. H2O.

Rise up

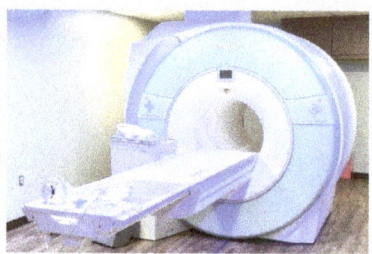

It's called Magnetic Resonance Imaging and I went to the appointment prepared to take a nap. Where some people are completely traumatized by the tight confines of the MRI machine I am not at all affected by claustrophobia. The device they are using today is a brand new one. It's smoother, quieter, a modern marvel with memory-foam pillows, headphones and you can choose your own musical playlist. Naptime. They laid me down on a table that will slide inside what looks like a small, metal tomb. They strapped me down to the table to prevent my moving during the procedure and the drawer slowly slid me into the cocoon. Within those few minutes of mesmerizing quiet as I lay there with my hands peacefully folded across my chest and my elbows tucked close to my sides I fell fast asleep. All of a sudden I heard that sound. Aaaannnnnkkkk! It was like a horn blowing inside that vibrates through the whole machine and into the metal table I was lying on. I jolted out of sleep trying to figure out where I was and what was going on? A few seconds and I remembered, "oh yeah, I'm in the MRI." Then this thought came to mind. "I wonder if this is what it's going to be like when the trumpet sounds and we are caught up to meet Him in the air?"

1 Thessalonians 4:16 says "For the Lord himself shall descend from heaven with a shout, with the voice of the archangel and with the trump of God: and the dead in Christ shall rise first:" What a promise! But Hold On that's not all. It gets even better in verse 17 "Then we which are alive and remain shall be caught up together with them in the clouds, to meet the Lord in the air: and so shall we ever be with the Lord." YES LORD, there it is, a reason, the reason, to keep holding on. It's not over yet. This is not the end. This life today is only a test and we are going to overcome it. Poverty, separation, pain, disease, divorce, addictions, hunger, disasters, wars, lies and yes death, even death will end at the trumpet sound. Our loved one's that went to sleep claiming the blood of Jesus and were laid to rest are just napping and at the trumpet sound they are going to rise up. So let's get ready to meet them by living like we believe. That's the promise He gave us. That's the hope He purchased with His blood. Won't you claim it with me right now? Today, is a good day, to just imagine that great day when that trumpet sounds and we will be reunited with all our loved ones. Until the New Jerusalem, Hold On.

HoldOn and Overcome. H2O

Of All Places

*A*s I drove through the gates entering the cemetery I thought back to a childhood experience. Once while driving by a place of rest my parents planted a seed of fear in my heart when they remarked that they would like to live, of all places, next to a cemetery. They joked that the people that live there would be the best neighbors and never bother anyone. The special effects of movies brought to my mind the horrifying scenes from Frankenstein, Dracula, Zombies and the others who took joy and residence in graveyards. Those memories were enough to cause sleepless nights at the thought of living, of all places, next to a cemetery. Please parents, have you no sense at all? But today, standing here in this cemetery I can't help but think that I would like to live, of all places, next to a cemetery. Just so I could see it.

That great morning of 1 Thessalonians 4:16,17, "For the Lord himself shall descend from heaven with a shout, with the voice of the archangel and with the trump of God: and the dead in Christ shall rise first: Then we which are alive and remain shall be caught up together with them in the clouds, to meet the Lord in the air: and so shall we ever be with the Lord."

Hold On Family, I want to see it. Don't you? I want a front row seat of all places, at the cemetery. So if we can just Hold On today we have the promise that we will be caught up in the clouds when Jesus comes back to get His resting saints and then those that are still alive who had a front row seat to see it all. Help us Jesus. Just imagine being caught up together and reunited with all the ones we've lost and missed throughout the ages and finally to live with them forever in, of all places, heaven. Believe, Pray, Try. Repeat and Hold On. Because it is as sure as He is on the throne. He *is* coming back for us and today, just may be a great day, to visit a cemetery and just imagine that great day.

HOLD ON. HOLDON 2 OVERCOME. H2O

Unprecedented

*I*n Genesis 22:2 Abraham is instructed by God to take his only son Isaac and sacrifice him as a burnt offering. This was actually a double death sentence. First, as the sacrifice Isaac was going to be cut with a knife and allowed to bleed to death then his body was to be burned on an open fire. If he survived the knife then he'd face the flames. Isaac and Abraham had performed this ceremony many times and they both knew that no sacrifice had ever survived or lived to tell about it. I've heard great sermons proposing that Abraham's faithfulness allowed him to believe that even if Isaac were killed God could bring him back from the dead but Abraham had not known anyone to come back from the dead and in this case two deaths. If the body was consumed by fire there wouldn't even be a body to resurrect. At this point in history there wasn't a Bible with the recorded accounts of God raising people from death. Abraham was stepping out on what was surely *unprecedented faith*.

See, we have the Word. We know that God can bring life from death because it is recorded that He did it for Lazarus. Abraham didn't have that. We have the Bible which tells us about those 3 Hebrew boys and so we know that flames don't always burn or consume but Abraham didn't have that. We have the knowledge written down for us about that ram in the thicket. Abraham hadn't experienced that yet. So there is faith in believing what is possible but unseen and there is unprecedented faith in hoping for something with no idea what the solution could even be. Adam experienced that in asking for a mate when no other human existed yet. Hold On Family, I propose today that with our God *all* things are possible so let Him worry about the how. When impossible becomes even more impossible. When God's messages to you, even His Word seems conflicting. When there literally is no way. When you think God is asking just too much. Hold On a little while longer because God, our God, has a plan for the knife and for the flames. When following God's instructions seems impossible, Hold On.

Today we have abundant access to all kinds of resources and information right in the palms of our hands and people love to check for references or search for reputable proof. All Abraham had that day was faith in his God. Faith to step out into the darkness and take hold of the unknown. Faith to believe and obey even when it's never been done before. Faith is unprecedented. Hebrews 11:1 says Faith is when you're hoping but just can't see it. So today I'm going to reach up and claim that promise and if it's never happened before then I'm willing to step out on my faith in my God that He will be with me when I'm the first one. Today, is a great day, for my *unprecedented miracle* so I'm Holding On.

HoldingOn 2 Overcome. How about you? H2O

Wait for Your 8

Most people have at least heard of the man named Job. Did you know that his story encompasses 42 chapters of the Bible and totals nearly 1,100 verses? It's true. I know because I counted them. In those 1,100 verses the account begins with some background information about Job and it is plainly apparent that Job is living the high life then there is a shift in the discourse between the roaming enemy satan and our God who is confident in the character of His faithful servant Job. The enemy issues a challenge and God allows Job to become the target of satan's evil intentions but with a constraint to just how far he could go in attacking him.(Job 1:12 and 2:6) This is a reminder that Jesus in grace and mercy still limits the enemy's attacks on us His children.

Starting with Job 1:13, Job is given terrible news of personal tragedies. He suffers through the losses of His business (but not his wealth, his home, his personal belongings, friends, or wife). He suffers through sickness and pain in his physical body. Job endures so much and for so long (a full year) that his story has become the standard and example for man's suffering. But then in Job 42:17 God ends the trials. God can and does rebuke and bind the enemy's permission and power to torment us. But the eventual restoration and double-harvest that most people focus their attention on are actually only recorded in the last 8 verses of the last chapter.

So why would God record 1,100 long verses of trials and only 8 short verses of triumph? I propose that it is because God knows that we will find Him in the valley not the victory, the trial and not the triumph! He looks for those willing to bear a cross in order to wear a crown. The race is given to him that endures to the end. The victory is in the finale.

Hold On Family, God wants us to focus not just on the blessings but on the one who does the blessing. He is telling us that we may have to go through 1,100 to get to the final 8. Yes, it could be difficult, take some time and even your friends and family may turn against you but God tells us in Hebrews 13:5 "I will never leave you nor forsake you." In this account of Job God is reminding us that He is with us and the trials are only temporary. Job is known for enduring the greatest tribulations but he is also known for the greatest restoration. God has a great restoration planned for each and every one of us, including me [*say your name*]. That great finale will be one day soon and I hope to meet Job in the New Jerusalem. Together we will walk and talk with Jesus on streets of gold beside the sea of glass. Until then, *wait for your 8* because today, is a great day, for restoration.

JUST HOLD ON. HOLDON 2 OVERCOME H2O.

The Other Side

John 21:4-6 "Early that morning Jesus stood on the shore of the Sea Tiberias but the disciples did not realize that it was Jesus they were looking at. He called out to them, "Friends, haven't you any fish?" They answered "No." He said, "Throw your net on the other side of the boat and you will find some." Jesus is talking to professional fishermen who were born and raised on this body of water but the fact remained that after they had exhausted every effort they still had nothing to show for it. Maybe in utter despair they concluded they had nothing to lose at this point so they carried the nets to the other side of the boat and threw them in. To their joy and amazement almost instantly the nets were filled with fish, so much so that they were unable to get the net back into the boat due to the weight of the fish.

Hold On Family, did you catch that? The breakthrough, the blessing and the harvest came… after. First, they were fishing, working, putting forth the effort. They were not at home, in church, or just praying about it. Breakthroughs take some effort. (Proverbs 10:4,5) Second, Jesus called them *friend*. There was an established relationship and recognition. (James 2:23 4:4) Can Jesus call you friend? Third, they answered Jesus. Do you recognize His voice? Are you spending time in His Word? Do you answer when He calls? (1Sam 3) Fourth, Jesus gives an instruction, *specific* for the desired outcome. It's going to take more than what you think (self-help ideology) or what you've always done (ceremonial worship). God ordains and then makes a way and we have to be able to differentiate His will from our desires. (Matt 6:33) Fifth, they took the time to listen. Breakthrough may require a pause. (Ps 27:14) We might have to stop what we are doing for a moment to focus our attention on what God is saying to us. This is the time for prayer and fasting. Maybe a specific covenant with God asking for a revelation or sign. (Judges 6:36-40) Sixth is obedience. They did exactly what Jesus told them to do. Breakthroughs require following directions. (John 14:15) And seventh is more work and effort. The fish are in the net but they have to get the fish to shore for the final harvest.

 Hold On by faith, but be ready and willing to make the effort and give it your best. Take time to establish that faith relationship. Spend time talking with Him in prayer. Listen for and to His specific instructions and then follow His directions. That's how you get your nets filled and to shore. God and His miracles are sure but we have to be willing to trust Him and follow His instructions even though they go against our knowledge, experience, or natural inclinations. For a breakthrough we have to be willing to try the *other side* because today, is a great day, to fill the nets.

HoldOn 2 Overcome. H2O.

Wrestling Giants

Some situations, problems and lessons are faced from a distance. David never actually *fought* Goliath. Actually, Goliath never even got close to David or laid a hand on him. That giant was handled and defeated from a distance but there are other times when we seem to find ourselves up close and personal in sweaty hand-to-hand combat with our giants. It may seem that even if the giant falls it will fall on us and crush us. We're holding the full weight of it all and can't break free from the strangle hold. Those times when it's not someone else feeling the struggles but *me* that's under the attack. When I lose a friend or loved one. When I am down to the last few quarters. When I have been laid off. When I have to see the doctor for the test results. When I have been mistreated and misrepresented. Yes, it's different when we have to wrestle the giants up close, getting down in the dirt and smelling their bad breath hitting us in the face.

But Hold On Family, there is a timely message for us today in 2 Chronicles 32:7-8 "Be strong and courageous. Do not be afraid or discouraged because of the king of Assyria and the vast army with him (the giant), for there is a greater power with us than with them. With him is only the arm of flesh, but with us is the Lord our God to help us and fight our battles. "And the people gained confidence ....." Yes, that is a quote from verse 8 and exactly what it says. "And the people gained confidence!" Hold On, close or far, I [*say your name*] am not alone in battling the giants. I have a mighty, powerful and wonderful warrior on my side. I have a tag-team partner that has never lost a match and He will help me fight my battles. So Hold On because today, is a great day, for me to gain confidence and see this giant in front of me fall.

HoldOn 2 Overcome. H2O.

Alternative Choice

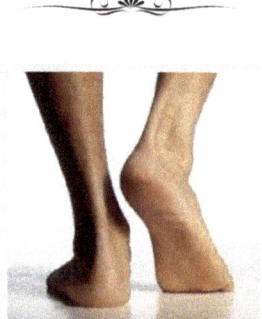

A friend relayed a story of determination. She had several things to do all in one day. She carefully laid out the plan, got up early and set out to be productive. She ran a few errands, dropped her car at the shop and got a ride to the Department of Motor Vehicles. That's where her plan was derailed. Her ride to get back home and then back to the car dealership couldn't make it. What to do? Without hesitation she told me she walked home. As I pondered and realized just how long that walk was I also realized she had said it with pride and without hesitation. She wasn't upset, letdown or bitter. No, she was proud of her accomplishment. She didn't let the situation dictate her outcome. I remarked, "Thank God for legs, because some people can't even walk." My friend replied, "Amen."

Hold On Family, whether you are sitting or standing right now take a moment and look down. Those two things with the shoes on them are the feet God supplied to make sure you have an alternative choice to being stuck anywhere that is if you are willing to walk. Take a look at your arms and follow them down to your hands and fingers. Those are the things you can always utilize as an alternative choice to being hungry, if you're willing to work. In between, just above those two feet you'll find two knees. God supplied those to offer an alternative choice for any and every situation you will ever encounter in your entire life if you are willing to get on those knees and *pray*. You always have a choice when you can pray. 2 Corinthians 5:7 says, "For we walk by faith, not by sight." So don't worry if your plans got derailed or if others may let you down. Just keep going. God has already supplied an alternative choice, a Plan B, another way, a comeback, a breakthrough and a victory. You can always walk, you can always work and yes you can always PRAY. Just Hold On, because today, is a great day, for a prayer and miracle.

JUST HOLDON 2 OVERCOME. H2O.

The Answer Is

If you've ever watched Family Feud the image of this scoreboard reveals what must surely be a record for dashed hopes and disappointments. It's a game show where two people try to match their responses to survey questions asked to 100 people in 5 categories and the goal is to get a combined 200 points. The first person did exceptionally well gathering 90% of the needed points. The second person comes out onto the stage and sees she only needed 18 points to win $20,000. Let the celebrations begin! Cakewalk, right? Five categories, five answers, surely out of 500 possible answers she can match 18. You see the scoreboard. 0,0, no answer, 0 and then... ZERO! Unbelievable. SMH. That poor woman is going to need a lot of therapy but Hold On Family, isn't that our lives too? So close but yet so far away.

Every day we are all trying to get the answers right and win the grand prize. Mark 8:36, 37 says, "For what shall it profit a man, if he shall gain the whole world and lose his own soul? Or what shall a man give in exchange for his soul?" The grand prize is sooo close, but... Ok, here's the solution. Colossians 3:23, 24, "Whatever you do, work at it with all your heart, as working for the Lord, not for human masters, since you know that you will receive an inheritance from the Lord as a reward. It is the Lord

Christ you are serving." The Hallelujah translation: Do your best, give it your all and take it to the Lord for help. He *will* be your answer. When you are a child of the King you can give the answer "JESUS" for every question you will ever encounter. All day, every day, the answer to every question, every dilemma, every decision is Jesus. Philippians 3:12-14 "....I press toward the mark for the prize of the high calling of God in Christ Jesus." There it is. What's the answer and the prize? The answer *is* the prize. JESUS. Press on, Hold On and just remember that you are not alone on this stage of life. You have family with you and behind you to help you win the game. No matter what the question, situation, challenge, or circumstance, you can't go wrong by answering with the name of Jesus. Cue the winning music track, the flashing lights, the audience applause, the victory dance. Today, is a great day, for the winning prize.

HoldOn 2 Overcome. H2O

Less is More

*S*omeone said to me once sometimes, less is more and I never forgot it. I wonder is it really? There is a Biblical truth recorded in both Matthew 19:24 and Mark 10:25 that can be applied here. In both texts the words are repeated, "It is easier for a camel to walk through the eye of a needle, than for a rich man to enter the kingdom of heaven." Is this saying that rich people won't be in heaven? Isn't it good to be rich? Aren't wealth, prosperity and the comforts of life things to be desired and sought after?

Certainly these texts do not say that rich people will not enter heaven but both texts say "easier" meaning that there is a logical comparison. If one is easier then the other is logically harder. It's harder to be rich and enter the kingdom of heaven. But why? 1Peter 6:6-8 speaks of being content with the necessities of life. Verse 9 begins to warn us how riches can bring temptations and snares and then verse 10 clarifies that it's not the money, but the *love* of money that can cause humans to stray and lose focus? Why? What does loving, wanting and pursuing money do to a person that could keep them out of heaven?

I propose there are two things to be aware of. Verse 10 says covet. Let's be clear that desire in itself is not bad but coveting is when we desire something so badly that we are willing to compromise on our principles to get it. If we are willing to break one of the other nine commandments like lie, steal, or kill it's coveting. In simple terms when you want something so badly that you will intentionally disobey God to get it, you're becoming a camel. Wealth has a tendency to change people. The more they get the more they want and the more they are willing to do to get it, good or bad and secondly is the word self. It's when we begin to take credit for what only God can do and when the power and the influence of the blessings start to outweigh the power and influence of Him who gives the blessings. What "I" accomplished by "my" hard work...." It's a shift in the balance and we tend to rely less on God and more on our efforts. Usually it starts with the less that we have (things) the more we need Him (Jesus) but as our circumstances improve we seem to not need prayer, patience and protection as much as before. The more we have (things) the less we need (Jesus), so more becomes less. The more we can do for ourselves the less we need Him to do for us but don't we all still need a Savior?

Remember the old Aesop's fable? Would you rather have a golden egg or the goose that lays the golden eggs? Would you rather have the stuff or the one who created everything? The Lord's Prayer as recorded in Matt 6:9-13 says "Give us this day our Daily Bread..... and lead us not into temptation, but deliver us from evil: For thine is the kingdom, power and the glory forever..." Our daily bread comes from the one who has the kingdom, the power and the glory. The Bible also tells us that it is impossible to serve two masters, God and mammon. (material wealth) We will love one and hate the other. (Luke 16:13). Hence the impossibility of getting a camel through the eye of a needle.

It all comes down to the simple decision of who and what we are going to love. John 3:16 "For God so loved the world that He gave....*everything*." Some of us will never be wealthy because God loves us, He knows us and He is trying to save us by not allowing anything to come between Himself and us. He gave up walking the streets of gold to come here and live a life of less, so that we could one day join Him to have it all. If having less right now means I have more of Jesus and that's what it takes to overcome, then I'll just Hold On and keep believing. Hold On and keep praying. "Lord, less of me and more of you." Today, is a great day, to receive more than I ever imagined from the creator of all.

HoldOn 2 Overcome. H2O

Rattled or Focused

We were discussing the recent World Cup win by the US Women's team and how various teams reacted when they were behind in the score. If you play sports sooner or later you're going to get scored on. There will be challenges and losses. Few people ever go without losing at one time or another. Not winning is a part of winning. So it's not that you lose, but how you handle it that makes champions.

Reading in the book of Joshua we find the writer literally whining and complaining about a setback. In chapter 7:7-9 right after the mighty walls of Jericho fell Joshua is actually asking God, "Why did you bring us across the Jordan River to be defeated by the enemy...?" After reading this don't you wanna just ask old Joshua what kind of question is that? Are you questioning God's whole plan? Was it better on the other side? Did He not bring you this far, allow you to cross a river and never got your feet wet and then brought down the impossible walls of Jericho without a fight?"

Hold On Family, God wants us to bring it to Him. He knows and understands our fears and frustrations and so He answers Joshua with a message that is quite appropriate for us today. The next time you feel like whining or complaining read Joshua 7:10 "The Lord said to Joshua, "Stand up! What are you doing down on your face?" Wow, first He orders Joshua to stand up and then He asks why was he down there in the first place? Why am I [*say your name*] down on my face? Am I going to let these challenges shake me so that I fall on my face complaining or am I going to stand up and get focused? The only reason to be down on my face is if I'm praying.

God says get up and I'll give you the solution and direction. Get up and I'll help you be victorious. So we have a choice today when we find ourselves behind in the score, we can get rattled or get up and get focused. Now read Joshua chapter 8 to see what God can and will do for us when we follow his direction. Get focused and be assured that today, is a great day, for a miraculous victory.

So Hold On. HoldOn 2 Overcome. H2O.

Eye on You

I just watched a news report about some kids who thought it would be funny to point and shine a laser at a helicopter flying overhead. Well that chopper turned out to be a police helicopter and those young people were about to learn the hard way that shining lights/lasers at flying aircraft is not funny at all. Actually, it's quite illegal. Even in the darkness of night and from way up there the police with their modern technology and special cameras were able to zoom in and see the kids in the backyard down to the details of their hair and clothing. In mere moments the police in the helicopter above radioed and sent police on the ground to the house and they arrested all the people there.

Job states in chapter 23:8,9 "But if I go to the east, he is not there; if I go to the west, I do not find him. When he is at work in the north, I do not see him; when he turns to the south, I catch no glimpse of him." Sometimes, like it is recorded here in Job's writings, it just seems like God is nowhere to be found. North, East, South, or West. We want to be faithful but just can't see or feel what we're supposed to Hold On to and then the enemy is whispering in our ears, talking trash, disparaging and discouraging. He wants us to feel alone and helpless. He loves to remind us of our mistakes and tries to get us to believe that when we aren't perfect God distances Himself from us, turns His back on us, leaves us to suffer because of our mistakes. Not surprising because the enemy is the father of all lies.

But Hold On Family, the reference from Job 23 records more in verse 10, "But he knows the way that I take; when he has tested me, I will come forth as gold." There is the revelation and assurance. Even when we can't see him, he *sees* us. He's up there looking down on every detail, down to the hair and clothing. During the tests of life He keeps us. He directs us. He protects us. He blesses us. He forgives us. He heals us. He provides for us and then He brings us out as gold. God has a night vision camera that reaches all the way from glory and He always has us in view. He sees us and he told us in Luke 12:7 that He even knows the number of hairs on our heads. No camera could get that close but Jesus can. Hold On brothers and sisters. His eye is on the sparrow and I know He watches over ME!

KEEP HOLDING ON TILL YOU OVERCOME. H2O

Just Call Me Faithful

*W*hat would God call me? It is recorded in the saga of Job Chapter 1:8. God says, "Have you considered my servant Job?... he is blameless and upright, a man who fears God and shuns evil." Those are God's actual words and a pretty powerful description of a man wouldn't you say? In Luke 10:30-37 there is the account of a Samaritan man who is forever immortalized when spoken of with the adjective "good." This Samaritan is the utmost example of compassion and love but what adjectives could be used to describe me? If I were to put my name in that sentence I am not sure that "blameless and upright" would be the first words to come to mind. Patient and long-suffering, maybe sometimes. Easily forgiving and righteous? Not so much. Comparatively speaking if someone had to use adjectives to describe us, we just may be in trouble. Thankfully God is not finished with me yet.

Genesis 5:24 which speaks about Enoch. A man God favored so much that He took him directly to heaven without experiencing death. "Enoch walked faithfully with God." Then Genesis 15:6 says "Abram believed the Lord and He credited it to him as righteousness." Hold On Family, we may be a long way from perfect, good, or righteous but with grace and mercy, maybe, just maybe Jesus can call me *faithful*. I want Him to be able to point to me as one who didn't give up but held on. I don't have to memorize the Bible to be special, I can just call His name. I don't have to offer long, eloquent prayers but just remember to talk to Him about everything. I don't have to worry about making wrong decisions if I ask Him first. I can stop fretting over perfection and just keep trying because Jesus has perfection covered for all of us and it's free for the asking.

The promise is that holding on will be credited as righteousness and Jesus takes care of the rest. He substitutes His goodness in place of our failures. He did what we couldn't and then gives us the credit for it like we did it ourselves. He actually sees us as "blameless, upright, fears God and shuns evil." Then He will repeat the words of Matthew 25:21,23 "...well done thou good and faithful servant. You have been faithful over a few things, I will make you ruler over many things. Enter thou into the joy of the Lord." Aren't those the words you want to hear Jesus say about you? Aren't those the words you want to hear Jesus say to you? Well Hold On. Today, all you have to do is try and He will call you faithful.

JUST HOLDON 2 OVERCOME. H2O

The Recipe

Flour, eggs, oil, baking powder, sugar, milk, salt, butter, yeast, water and an oven. How many different dishes could you make? A little bit of this and a little bit of that, with a pinch here and a dash there you could have biscuits, pasta, doughnuts, pancakes, dumplings, a cake perhaps. It just depends on what combinations you put together with the ingredients at hand. Once you start learning to cook and get the hang of understanding how each ingredient affects the other and hence the final tasty outcome you will find yourself needing recipes less and less. You'll begin to feel it and just know instinctively how much sugar makes it sweet.

Hold On Family, I propose the same for your walk of faith. You really don't need every single recipe, solution, or answer ever written. Instead, what God gives us are the ingredients. We have containers full of life lessons, joys and tears, trials and victories along with the measuring tools of grace and mercy. There's a Master Chef's Manual separated into Old and New instructions and a whole family of excellent chef's to consult if need be.

Now picture Jesus standing there in your kitchen wearing an apron with batter on it, His sleeves rolled up and one of those white chefs hats on his head leaning to the side. Yes, He's got flour on his smiling face and an oven mitt on one hand. You notice the scar on the other hand as he takes your hand to guide you in stirring what's in the bowl before you. Proverbs 4:11-13. "I have taught thee in the way of wisdom; I have led thee in right paths. When thou goest, thy steps shall not be straightened; and when thou runnest, thou shalt not stumble. Take fast hold of instruction; let her not go: keep her; for she is thy life." Hold On, that's the recipe for life! Now read Psalms 34:8 "O taste and see that the Lord is good: blessed is the man that trusteth in him." Let's get cooking in the kitchen with our Master Chef and prepare something wonderful with the assurance that everything He makes turns out good. Today, is a great day, to feast at the welcome table and the bill is already paid.

Hold On, Hold On, HoldOn 2 Overcome. H2O.

Idle Angels

Could you imagine a scene in heaven where Jesus would have to get up from His throne because something just doesn't feel right? It's unusually quiet all around the heavenly court so Jesus goes looking for the angels to find out what's going on? He heads to the break-room and upon entering He sees countless messenger angels just standing around seemingly bored. There are angels gathered around the water cooler chit chatting and others standing in groups sipping heavenly nectar from invisible glasses. Some angels are reclining back on their folded wings and others are sitting on mounds of gold with their feet propped up on ottoman-sized jewels. Jesus is almost confused and inquiries in a voice only heard in heaven, "What's going on here fellas? Why aren't you all out there bringing the prayers from earth to the throne?" All the angels look back and forth sheepishly at each other of course not wanting to disappoint Jesus Himself. After a few awkward moments the mighty Gabrielle himself stands, clears his throat and turns to face his creator and reports, "Father, there just aren't any prayers coming up."

Hold On Family, that won't be the case as long as I'm living and breathing. If I don't receive a miracle today it won't be for lack of asking. John 14:13,14 "And whatsoever ye shall ask in my name, that will I do, that the Father may be glorified in the Son. If ye shall ask anything in my name, I will do it." Now read verse 15 for the clarification part. There is always a choice and a condition. Jesus says, If you love me, follow me." Brothers and sisters, I want all the angels buzzing back and forth, zipping up and down, flashing to and fro with my prayers. There won't be any idle angels with me alive and praying. I'm going to ask, ask again, ask some more and I won't stop asking until there's a breakthrough. Those angels will be tired and worn out before I'm finished. Protection, Peace, Love, Justice, Restoration, Family.... BREAKTHROUGH. Join me and let's fill heaven with our petitions. In Jesus' name, "Come boldly to the throne of grace, that we may obtain mercy and find grace to help in the time of need." Hebrews 4:16. Today, is a great day, for that answer from above.

HoldOn 2 Overcome. H20.

Creator Prepare

Consider this. Maybe I haven't experienced the breakthrough yet... maybe I haven't fulfilled the promise yet... maybe I haven't met with my destiny yet because it doesn't exist yet and we can't receive it if it's not ready to be received. Here is the message He sent me to share with you reading this right now. "The creator is *preparing me*, while He is *creating it*. The texts in Psalms 107:36,37 says "And there he maketh the hungry to dwell, that they may prepare a city for habitation; And sow the fields and plant vineyards, which may yield fruits of increase." It said prepare for habitation. Sow seeds, to yield fruit. I'll put it another way- God has me in a holding pattern while He prepares the landing field.

Our mighty and wonderful Father is creating the job, preparing the mate and working out the restoration. He's arranging the reunion, setting up the comeback and solving the problems. He's reshaping and restoring while simultaneously placing me at the right place at the right time to meet my destiny. Isaiah 40:28 tells us that "God, the Lord, is the creator of the *ends* of the earth." Hold On Family, when He finishes it, He will place you with it. If you need a reminder of His creative power and organizational genius just read Genesis chapter 1 and

2 to review how He created the heavens and prepared the Garden of Eden for Adam and Eve. He's doing the same thing right now for you and I. It's just a matter of time and every second brings us closer to that breakthrough that He is preparing. So keep praying, expect it and get ready for it.

BECAUSE ANY DAY NOW, YOU *WILL* OVERCOME. H2O.

"THIS" "THE" "AN" "CAN" "WILL"

This answer that I just received is not *the* answer that I had prayed for, but it's still *an* answer revealing that God did hear me and He *can* and *will* answer the rest of my prayers. This occurrence, this thing that just happened, this call that just came was undoubtedly an answer from God and there is just no other way to explain it. There isn't and then there is? There wasn't and then there was? A way out of no way appears and I know I just witnessed a miracle. Yet while I'm not trying to sound ungrateful I just know there is more to come. I asked for and claimed the promise of a complete answer to my prayer and this is only a partial breakthrough. This turn of events is encouraging and surely a sign but it is still a fragmented piece of the big picture. I just can't help but ask God what about the whole request? What about the bigger picture and the complete answer?

Hold On Family, the message to you today is *an* answer, *any* answer, no matter how small is God telling you, "Hold On my child, keep calling my name and I will finish what I started with you." Let's personalize Psalms 91 by reading the H2O version and inserting your own names in the following blank spaces of verse 14, 15.

"Because _____ hath set his/her love upon me, therefore will

I deliver _____: I will set _____ on high, because _____ hath known my name. _____ shall call upon me and I will answer : I **will** be with _____ in trouble; I will deliver _____ and honor _____."

That's how we claim a personal promise. Take God's own words and repeat them back to Him. Go right ahead and place your name in it and Hold On because *this* is only the first answer, it is not *the* final answer. There is still *an* answer to come that *can* and *will* fulfill it all. Read your personal Psalms 91 a few more times until you begin to believe it.

Now keep praying and HoldOn 2 Overcome. H2O

Believe is an Action Word

*I*f you open the Bible and start counting you will find that the word *believe* occurs 143 times in 131 separate verses. If you open a dictionary it says that this word believe is a verb, an action word. The official definition is to "accept (something) as true, feel sure of the truth of." It's a simplistic definition but boy does it carry some weight. On the face of it the concept of *believe* is the basis, the backbone, the foundation of and for faith. In order to have faith, practice faith, Hold On to faith you first have to *believe* in something. We all *believe*. Most of us get up early in the morning, dress and then drive to some place of employment where we put forth some effort we call work because we *believe* at the end of one of those weeks they are going to hand us a check or deposit some money in a bank account with our name on it. We don't ask every day if it's payday but we *believe* that day is coming and so we keep going to work.

Believe is a by-product of choice and conversely if we had only one alternative and no other possible scenarios we really wouldn't have to *believe* at all. With only one possible outcome our lives would be mundane day to day cycles of predestiny but since we are given choices man has come up with quite a list of possibilities for where he came from, how he exists in the world and what happens after this life is over. God loves us and He allows us to choose and answer the question for ourselves of what we *believe*. Was it a cosmic big bang or was it God's creation? Is there really a God in heaven? Does He love me? Why is there suffering? Did He really come to save me? Is He coming back again?

If you have ever heard a voice speaking in the back of your mind that you knew was leading you in the right direction. If you have felt a comforting presence that you couldn't quite explain. If you have been completely without hope and then something just happened to shift things in your favor. If you know you have stared death in the face and lived to tell about it. If the scientific evidence just doesn't add up and still leaves too many unanswered questions. If you were caught in the iron grip of some addiction, spinning out of control, headed for disaster and then cried out in desperation for another chance and have been clean and sober ever since… then you b*elieve*. You accept it. You know it is true and feel sure of it.

Hold On Family, *believe* that we are all struggling to *believe* but we are going to make it. Just a few more moments and any day now. The last Biblical *believe* is found in 1 John 5:13 which reads: "These things have I written unto you that *believe* on the name of the Son of God; that ye may know that ye have eternal life and that ye may *believe* on the name of the Son of God." Beyond whether we *believe* in Him or not what we do know for sure is that He *believed* and still *believes* in us. He took action, the ultimate action, by giving His life. Hold On Family, that's the message. Now all we have to do to *believe* is to accept it and act as if it were true.

Try this. Take a quiet moment to just bow your head and whisper it, "I *believe*." Close your eyes for a minute and repeat it a few times, "I *believe*, I *believe*, I *believe*." Now *believe* that He heard you because today, is a great day, to *believe* in miracles.

BELIEVE 2 OVERCOME. B2O

The Technique

This was an assignment/questionnaire for my daughter's seventh grade health class. It was entitled "Skills for Managing Stress" and these were some of the questions that were asked. When I have too much to do, I usually___? When I make a mistake, I usually___? When I am very late for something, I usually___? When I am really angry with someone I care about, I usually___? When I can't do something I want to do, I usually___? When I lose something that is important to me, I usually___? Then the assignment said "Look over your responses and identify what techniques you use most often to deal with stress?"

Hold On Family, there are days when we encounter one of these situations and there are days when we face them all plus a few more. The question is, "What techniques do I use?" Sometimes I just close my eyes and whisper, "Father God, Lord in Heaven, sweet Jesus please help me right now." Then I feel a breeze caused by the angel's wings as they rush to my side. Psalms 5:2 "Hear my cry for help, my King and my God, for to you I pray." It put a smile on my face and a warmth in my heart when I read how my daughter had answered her question. She had simply written, "I pray." Today I am here to remind you that our God is a stress reliever. He *is* the technique. For all the problems, dilemmas, scenarios and complications. For every question, He has the answer. From A to Z, one to one zillion, infinity and beyond just call on His name.

I am utterly convinced that the source of all stress and anxiety is the enemy and his demonic hosts of helpers.(John 10:10) Someone changed my life years ago by stating the absolute and undeniable fact that "the devil can't be in the presence of God's praise." With that knowledge in mind I'd like to share my simple but effective go-to method/prescription for stress relief. Give God some **praise** and to help set the atmosphere I keep inspirational music playing continually and especially while I sleep at night. (1 Samuel 16) I have several special playlists that I keep on standby to serve as weapons of warfare for different situations. I'd be more than happy to share some great music choices for lifting spirits and invoking peace. First put on your music and stop whatever you are doing for a few quiet moments to relax and start giving thanks. Begin by looking at one of your hands and then say thank you God for this hand. Now think of the things that would be different in your life if you didn't have this one hand. Then move to your thumb and repeat the process. Say thank you Lord for this thumb and then think of some things that would be different in your life if you didn't have this thumb. Repeat for every finger that you have and then start moving up to the arm. How would your life be different if you didn't have your right arm? Your left shoulder, your right shoulder, your neck and on to the head. Say Thank you Father for my left eye. Think about how my life would be different without this eye. Both eyes, hair, eyebrows, eyelashes, ears, cheeks, teeth, lips, jaws and chin, don't leave anything out. Now you repeat this process "as needed until the symptoms of stress are reduced." If need be move beyond your body to your family members and then any and everything you can possibly think of to be thankful for. With some practice this technique is guaranteed to send evil spirits running for cover.

David knew it and he testifies to it in Psalms 42:9-11. When you begin praising and counting blessings the enemy can't stand it and he will leave carrying his stress with him. Read. Acts 16:24-26 where Paul and Silas got to singing and praying while imprisoned. Then read 2 Chronicles 20:22 and see what happened with singing and praise.

Hold On. You are not helpless. You have some stress relief methods that are sure and today, is a great day, to practice your technique.

HOLD ON 2 OVERCOME. H2O

IF YOU WOULD LIKE TO ENJOY AND SHARE OUR H2O PLAYLIST, VISIT our Youtube channel H2O Holdon 2 Overcome. If there is a selection that really speaks to your heart please leave a comment.

Fear-Less

    *D*o you remember your first time stepping off the end of the high diving board? How about riding a big roller coaster or holding a large snake in your hands? Do you have the nerve to parachute out of an airplane or could you walk across a glass-bottomed bridge? All these situations will require confronting fear itself. To help reduce our own levels of fear we could practice, purchase the best equipment and reassure ourselves by watching other people do it first. But Hold On Family, we know that there are some things that we just can't prepare for and so when confronted with these situations we are usually stopped dead in our tracks by fear.

    So today I propose that we endeavor to fear…less. Now that doesn't mean that we won't ever worry or be afraid. There are times and reasons when fear is useful and can actually save us. No, we are not talking about being fearless as in the absence of all fear. What I'm talking about right now is fearing LESS in the presence of the threat. In the middle of the storm when the bills are twice your paycheck and your bank account is overdrawn. When facing a layoff and a possible eviction at the same time. When we are walking towards the giant threatening to crush our bones or if we are being lowered into a den of hungry lions. For those who may be dreading the treatment for the diagnosis that was given. I'm not without fear but I'm going to give some of that fear to God for Him to hold for me. Let Him hold it in His hands because He is able.

Consider this statement. *Yes, there is reason to fear, but I don't have to fear it because whatever it is that I fear, fears my God.* Just repeat that until it sinks in and begins to make sense. Just repeat and remember that "my God is greater!" Psalm 118:6 tells us, "The Lord is on my side; I will not fear: what can man do unto me?" Proverbs 29:25 repeats, "The fear of man bringeth a snare: but whoso putteth his trust in the Lord shall be safe."Hold On and fear *less*." Lord, thank you. Now help us to trust in you and fear LESS knowing you are with us and are greater than anything we will ever encounter. We claim it in the name of Jesus, Amen." Hold On because it is a fact. Today, is a great day, to become fear-less.

JUST HOLDON 2 OVERCOME. H2O.

Go in Peace

You may have heard that saying about "peace in the midst of the storm." In Acts 16:25 we find Paul and Silas imprisoned, wrongfully accused and even physically beaten. Yet it is recorded, "And at midnight Paul and Silas prayed and sang praises unto God: and the prisoners heard them sing praises." They were literally singing praises in the midst of the storm but I propose that there is more to be realized here. Verse 26 says "And suddenly there was a great earthquake, so that the foundations of the prison were shaken: and immediately all the doors were opened and everyone's bands were loosed."

Let's examine this chapter a little closer. First, after their prayers they were miraculously freed. Second, verse 33 says "And he took them the same hour of the night and washed their stripes; "The pain they had been suffering was relieved and the healing began. Third, verse 34 says "And when he had brought them into his house, he set meat before them." Now they are fed, filled and satisfied. That which once was empty like bank accounts, promises, homes and minds are now full. Fourth is found in verse 36, "The magistrates have sent to let you go: now therefore depart and go in peace." They now experienced freedom, release and peace. As escaped prisoners they would have had to look over their shoulders and fear recapture for the rest of their lives but now they are set free legally and are restored as vindicated and respectable citizens with the hope of living a peaceful life thereafter.

Hold On Family, I say that if we are going to pray for something from this great, all-powerful and omnipotent God let's ask for Him to end the storm! "Jesus, thank you. Now please roll back the clouds, bring out the sun and let's go to the beach." Yes family, you can pray for peace if you want to but my God is bigger than that. Jesus that day standing in that boat on that storm-tossed sea didn't speak peace for the men in the storm, no sir. He spoke peace to the storm! Have mercy! Some pray, some chant and others may meditate for peace but I'm calling my God on His word to set me free to enjoy peace. Heal me, fill me and restore me! The Word also says, "You have not because you ask not," and today I need a victory so I pray, "Yes Lord, I need peace right now. I need to be freed, healed, filled and restored and I claim it in the mighty name of Jesus, Amen." Now we just have to Hold On and never stop claiming the victory. For today, is a great day, to receive *peace*.

JUST HOLDON 2 OVERCOME. H20

The Little Things

Last night I was tired and dirty...*really* dirty. After a morning run I went directly to help someone install a garage door opener and so I was covered in sawdust and wood chips from cutting overhead. This didn't help my back any which was already sore from a previous fall off a ladder. Then someone walking by lost control of their pet and called out to me for help so I had to chase, catch and wrestle with a stinky dog. When I was finally standing in the shower so ready for the sweet relief of hot water and there was.... NO SOAP! Oh no! I knew there was something I was supposed to get earlier. In desperation I searched high and low and behold in my travel bag I found one of those little complimentary hotel bars of soap. You would have thought I found gold. At that moment I was reminded to be thankful for the little things.

Take a moment and imagine your life without soap? How would life be different without one thumb or big toe? Even though you have two eyes and ears, what if one were missing? What if the toilet didn't flush or the refrigerator didn't cool? How about those headlights and windshield wipers on a rainy day? The cell phone, the wallet, the keys you lost and found. Hold On and take a moment to .....1, 2, 3, 4, 5, 6, 7, ...just count your blessings. Psalms 34:8 invites us to "Taste and see that the Lord is good." Luke 16:10 says, "He that is faithful in little, is faithful in much" which directly applies to "He that is thankful in little, is thankful in much." It was just a little piece of soap but it sure made a big difference. "Thank you Lord for all the little things that remind us to Hold On." If you're ever unsure, tired or wondering if anybody cares at all just start counting because today is a great day to realize that I am really blessed even by the little things.

So I'll keep holding on. HoldOn 2 Overcome. H2O.

There Will Be Days

I was driving and a vehicle pulls up right next to mine. The driver's window rolls down and I hear my name called. I recognized the female driver even though I hadn't seen her in a while. She looked a little different. I asked, "How are you?" Her eyes began to tell a tale. Sometimes people need some uplifting and sometimes people need some listening. We need to learn how to interpret which is which. Maybe listen first then give the advice. This woman is a single mom of 3 small children and she's trying to work more than one job while dealing with a tumultuous relationship. Life gets tough sometimes with nobody to just talk to. We parked and I got out of my car and walked over to her ready to lend an ear. I stood at her driver door and noticed the bottle of alcohol next to her on the seat. She noticed that I must have seen it and she just blurted out, "Don't judge me, I'm on the edge." She shared and I had to agree with her that things in her life sounded a little crazy at the moment. She said everything had gotten so bad that she could barely cope. Then she pointed to the suitcase in the back seat and said that it was packed and next to it was another bottle in a little paper bag.

She had been doing so well on the road to sobriety but it's quite common for people that "used to drink" to start drinking again and people that "used to smoke" to start smoking again. Old habits can come back with a vengeance, more aggressive and even more destructive than before. All the "used tos" like over-eating, under-eating, the wrong crowds and places, the booze, needles, pills and the powder. The morning after morning of regret and shame can all come back to haunt us when we least expect it.

There will be days when people pack bags and bottles. You better believe that the enemy doesn't want you to just drink. He has a bigger plan in mind. He wants you to be driving while intoxicated and be the cause of a terrible accident that injures some innocent people. The enemy is constantly plotting how he can bring about a disaster in your life to cause enough stress so that you will revert back to the old bad habits. He wants you to self-medicate and drown your sorrows to escape reality. He wants you to smoke herbs that came from the earth because they are natural and have healing benefits, right or maybe take some of those pain pills from the hospital which are not supposed to be addictive. That old devil just loves to apply misery in layers.

The enemy, he bowls. He knows that if he can hit the first pin (that's you and I) just right then the others will fall. The enemy sees and plans these elaborate webs of misfortune but he can't get past God's protection. (Job 2:6) What the enemy needs, plans and orchestrates is for you to step outside the fortress of God's defenses, take the bait of pleasure and/or self-preservation and get the ball rolling towards your own self destruction. If I [*say your name*] fall, my children fall, my family falls, my friends fall, it all falls. The enemy can make plans for my future but I know who sees the future and then brings it to pass. That's the comfort, the assurance, the strength to Hold On to. No matter the situation or the slip-up God can and will fix it.

Jeremiah 29:11 assures us that "I know the plans I have for you declares the Lord. Plans to prosper you and not to harm you. Plans to give you hope and a future. Now read Philippians 1:6; Romans 15:13; Proverbs 3:5,6; I Peter 1:3,4; 2 Corinthians 4:17,18; Lamentations 3:21-23; Proverbs 16:1-4 ; James 4:13-17 Psalms 103:1-5; Romans 8:18-25; Matthew 6:25-34. That's quite a few times God Himself is telling me [*say your name*] that even on my worst kinds of days, He is *still* there for me, arms open wide.

My friend and I talked for a long while in that parking lot and then we prayed. She is still alive today and since that time she has a better job, her children are doing well, she isn't drinking *and* she has gotten married. Just a little praise report for someone that may need it today. Remember there will be days, crazy days and then there will be days, for miracles and breakthroughs.

So HoldOn 2 Overcome. H2O.

The Handoff

It's football season again and for those who love to spend hours sitting down with their face glued to one screen or another, it's wondrous. Most people know the goal of the game is to make a touchdown by catching or carrying the ball into the end zone. The quarterback signals to put a play in motion and then those words, "Hike, Hike," are heard setting of a chain reaction. He looks to throw the ball to his receiver downfield for a score so he drops back and scurries left and right to avoid those huge, bloodthirsty defensive players that are attacking with bad intentions. Sometimes it's not the big plays that win the game but instead the small advances gained by something referred to as the *handoff*.

Do you see it Hold On Family? Have you been there? Maybe you're there now facing the impending sack. Well rather than be trampled by the approaching attackers, hand it off. Just pray, "Lord, I can't. You can, so please TAKE IT!" Then, like the quarterback, raise your hands towards heaven signaling you have passed it on. Sometimes we just need to "G.I.T.H," Give It To Him. No fumbles. Place your cares in the hands of the most capable scorer and Hold On. Right now all it takes is a whisper, "Jesus, help me!" Psalms 55:22 "Cast thy burden upon the Lord and he shall sustain thee: he shall never suffer the righteous to be moved." 1 Peter 5:7 says "Cast all your care upon him; for he careth for you." Hold On, hand off. Hold On and G.I.T.H. then be assured Jesus has a playbook and more wins than anyone.

So Hold On 2 Overcome. H2O.

Do the Math

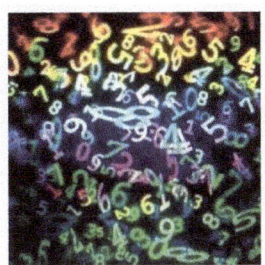

There are 365 days in a year. Just imagine how many times each day you've been saved, spared, or snatched from the jaws of death? How many times a day, whether you know it or acknowledge it, are you blessed? Now multiply that number times 365. Suppose you are blessed at least once an hour then that makes at least 8760 blessings a year. If you can imagine that you receive one blessing every 5 minutes then that is 105,120 blessings that came your way in the last year alone. Really, is it impossible to believe that a single minute goes by that God doesn't instruct an angel to divert an accident or calamity from your path? Is there a single minute that God is caught off guard? A solitary moment in time when the enemy has control over your destiny? What single second does Jesus leave the throne?

Hold On Family, I propose that there isn't a supercomputer produced yet that can begin to calculate the number of times in a day that we receive blessings, grace or mercy. Jeremiah 33:3 says "Call unto me and I will answer thee and shew thee great and mighty things, which thou knowest not." This verse confirms it again that we may not even know when He is interceding for us. We aren't even aware of what's taking place in the atmosphere above our heads but trust and believe every millisecond of every hour of every year, of every decade our God is working it out. Constantly. 24/7 and 365 days a year. We should constantly be saying thank you.

"Thank you Lord for all the blessings too numerous to count. Now we ask you to lead on, protect on and bless on in the days to come and we claim it in the name of Jesus, Amen." There is a song that says, "the Lord is blessing me right now, oh right now. He woke me up this morning and started me on my way. The Lord is blessing me, right now." The blessings will keep adding up until our Savior comes through the clouds to take us home. Do the math to remember and Hold On.

HoldOn 2 Overcome. H2O.

Strengthening Therapy

I remember the first time I went to physical therapy. It was after a car accident that I was prescribed treatment to supposedly help relieve the discomfort, restore my range of motion and allow me to again live the active lifestyle that I had been enjoying. The stretching, the moist heat pack on my back, and the tingle of electro stimulation were all part of the treatment. I had arrived expecting a nice massage and maybe a peaceful sauna treatment but these people had me working while I moaned, groaned and perspired. I really wanted to feel better so I was willing to try anything but when the therapist handed me those little pink dumbbells, maybe 5 pounds each, I had to ask her, "What are these supposed to do? All this equipment in here and you hand me, this big strapping man, these little pink lady weights? Don't you know I am a weight lifter? Don't insult me, give me some real weight!"

Have you ever questioned God and His methods? Can you just imagine the Children of Israel hearing the instructions for marching around the walls of Jericho? On many occasions I've had to ask the Lord why? Why me? What purpose will these petty struggles, ridiculous attacks and annoying ailments possibly serve in my life? Lord, this is really a waste of time... but let's consider if it actually is.

The strongest man that ever lived prayed in Judges 16:28 "And Samson called unto the LORD and said, O Lord God, remember me, I pray thee and strengthen me, I pray thee...." Hold On Family, if Samson needed strengthening how about us? Jeremiah 12:5 says "If you have run with the footmen and they have wearied you, Then how can you contend with horses? And if in the land of peace, In which you trusted, they wearied you, Then how will you do in the floodplain of the Jordan?" Well if Samson and the mightiest soldiers needed strengthening therapy, we all need it.

God's treatment plan doesn't just restore us back to our past condition, no sir. His treatment is going to make us bigger, better and stronger than ever before. God is striving to make us new creatures all together. Hold On and consider that the problems we face are actually a strengthening workout. The challenges are actually regenerative treatments and you are not alone. Isaiah 41:10 commands that we, "Fear thou not; for I am with thee: be not dismayed; for I am thy God: I will *strengthen* thee; yea, I will help thee; yea, I will uphold thee with the right hand of my righteousness." What a promise that is for us today. Say it with me, "I [*say your name*] am getting stronger. God is just restoring me and making me stronger." Repeat it and Hold On.

HoldOn 2 Overcome. H2O

Help/Hope

Titi Branch, co-founder of Miss Jessie's natural hair care line, dead at 45
washingtonpost.com

In the news is a prominent young woman's suicide. These reports of people attempting and far too often actually succeeding in taking their lives are ever increasing these days. Recently my own good friend traveled down a road with no return and I wondered and I questioned and I miss him. I also very well know what it feels like to not want to feel anything any more. Even when the sun is shining and there appears to be success, finances, beauty, possessions... it still just isn't enough for some people to keep dealing with the darkness. Please consider something I personally have come to realize. Most people do not want to die. The average person if attacked in a dark alley would fight for their lives but on some days the pressure, the pain, the hopelessness, the perceived weight of defeat and despair can just become too much to carry any longer. Depression whether diagnosed or disguised can become so heavy that even an overachiever can stop wanting to continue the struggle. Living becomes suffering and the suffering is just too much. Not being able to face tomorrow if it's going to be another day of feeling like this. After rest and peace have faded so far from view that the idea of "sleep" could seem a very attractive and welcome alternative to staying awake and in pain.

That's where friends, *real* friends, could come in. It seems that *after* a tragedy people talk and visit and ...regret. But what about before? The signs, the messages, the things that just didn't seem right or add up? I propose today that we all know somebody that's struggling and they may not be who we usually think they are. Oftentimes troubled people hide their troubles and become very adept at pretending to be OK. They too are the wealthy people, the people in front, the musicians leading the songs, or the perfect student. They may even be the people that help us like the police officers, the teachers, the soldiers and our neighbors, maybe even your doctor or dentist. There is no category or demographic that does not need a *real* friend.

Let's ask the real tough questions to deal with a real tough subject. Are some of us, sometimes, so busy doing us that we miss what could be cries for help? Are we sometimes so consumed in self and engrossed in progress that we can't be there for them? Who honestly would take a few days off from work to go sit with that friend? Who could drop everything just to let a friend know someone cares for them just that much. Often people don't talk because they feel no one really cares enough to try to understand them anyway. Loneliness is a diagnosable illness and the prescription is Love. Cook some food, take it over, wrap them in a blanket and just hold them. It goes for men as well because men need hugs too. Sometimes a *real* friend is defined by actions. So the question may be what would you do to save a friend's life if you knew their life was in danger?

I challenge myself and every one of us to give help and hope every day of the week. Do you know someone that has had a difficult time recently? Send a card with a few bucks in it, a gift card or a bouquet of flowers but better yet is for you to take the time to find out if your friends are really OK. Don't be too busy to make that visit or call. Maybe whisper a prayer over their life. Matthew 25:45 says "Then shall he answer them, saying, Verily I say unto you, Inasmuch as ye did it unto one of the least of these, ye did it into me." Hope saves lives and we can be that hope. No it's not guaranteed and we won't catch them all but it's worth trying for that one that could be saved.

HOPE ON 2 OVERCOME. H2O

The Fixer

I'm driving and it's raining hard. Visibility is reduced and traffic is slowing to a crawl. The obvious thing to do is to turn on the windshield wipers and to my annoyance there's that right wiper flopping around again. I was supposed to fix that a long time ago. The problem is I only think about it when it's raining and I can't see. Matthew 5:45 "That you may be children of your Father in heaven. He causes his sun to rise on the evil and the good and sends rain on the righteous and the unrighteous."

Hold On Family, isn't it easy to judge other people and think that their problems are their own doing and necessary for them to learn a lesson? We often forget that we all need the rain in our lives sometimes to remind us of what needs fixing. For windshield wipers it's an easy solution and we can head to the nearest auto parts store but for the tempest in our lives we head to the throne of grace for a shelter in the time of storm. We can fix windshield wipers but do you know who fixes hearts and minds? The One who takes away the taste for cigarettes, drugs and alcohol. The One who hears your prayers and takes that wayward child on a path to destruction and turns them around. The One who allows you to see the good in people and helps you control your tongue. The One who heals relationships and restores marriages.

Do you know there are some things that need fixing in your life? Well, it's quite simple, just ask Him. "Lord, today I thank you for the experiences which serve to remind me that I need fixing too. I give you permission to come in and work on my life. Please give me the strength and patience I need to go through this process and make me the person you meant for me to be. In the name of Jesus, Amen."

Don't be too hard on yourself. We all are human and you just took the first step towards a breakthrough. Your past has been erased and you have a fresh start so Hold On and expect a change. Today, is a great day, to get to know the Fixer.

So, Hold On 2 Overcome. H2O

Seek Means Try

The book of Amos is not exactly easy reading. It goes on and on about punishment, vengeance, wars, storms, death and destruction. You can't help but notice that the book of Amos, written thousands of years ago, sounds just like the evening news broadcast today does it not? Yet right there smack dab in the middle of all this strife and misery this simple truth is written in Amos 5:4, "This is what the Lord says to Israel: *seek me* and live." So simple but important enough to repeat it again in verse 6 "seek the Lord and live."

Hold On Family, it's a simple choice each one of us has to make. The text doesn't speak of earning it. It doesn't require that we attain any great level of righteousness. There's no time limit. No minimums or maximum requirements. No dollar amount. All it takes is to *try*. The text says, "seek" which means make an effort, look for, call upon, ask. Seek me means try me. Where did we get the notion that to have a relationship with God we have to be perfect or even good for that matter. How did the process get so complicated? Who says Jehovah is not a loving and caring God that wants all the best for us? So right now, with head bowed but fist upraised I invite you to declare with me today, "I [*say your name*] need you Lord and I claim your promises for my life and the lives of my loved ones."

Yes, it can be just that simple and right now in the midst of it all you can Hold On with confidence that you will receive an answer. You will live, laugh, love and overcome because today you chose Him and you called on Him and that's all He ever asked. Now Hold On for dear life and more abundantly.

HoldOn 2 Overcome. H2O

Who You Gonna Call?

      I clicked on the video link expecting to hear and learn some deep historic truth. I'd read and listened to the speaker many times before and had considered him a knowledgeable authority but this time something didn't feel right. What was it that He just said? Something about believing in the Bible is foolish? Allegory upon allegory? Did he just say that if you want to know the real history you should read the Egyptian manuscripts? Really? Well, great man of knowledge and wisdom, I have a question for you. "Who you gonna call, Ghostbusters?" If the ancient Egyptians were so smart, omnipotent, or omniscient, where are they now? How can the Egyptians help if the doctors say cancer? When that truck is barreling towards you out of control? When there's not enough to pay the bills? When the pain of grief is too much? Oh learned man, who do you know that knows it all? What promises do you Hold On to when you need a miracle? Who you gonna call that still answers today?

    Proverbs 30:5 "Every word of God is pure: he is a shield unto them that put their trust in Him." Amen. Hold On Family, I tell you that this man's statement that was intended to disparage a faith in God actually encouraged and multiplied my faith because I know neither the books nor the dead that wrote them have any power today. But there *is* a book, a living Word. It's a gift from God, the living God, that I can still call on today and receive a specific answer.

How do I know? Because I have tried and tested it for myself, over and over again. The fact that I am living and breathing at all today is a testimony that there is a God, a real God, because that is who I called on to save me when I could not save myself. I tried some other things and called some other names but none of them answered me. I read and studied some history but the more I learned the less it made sense. I tried to find happiness but it always came with a negative side effect. So I decided to try it and ask Him. I decided to test Him and wait. I said it out loud, "If you are real God, show me." You know what? He answered. Not like I thought it would be or even what I wanted but some things began to change. I experienced it for myself and that is the only way you are going to ever know. You have to try Him, for yourself.

So today when I might hear someone speak unkind things about my God or religion I am not at all upset. I just know they don't know Him, they are still fighting Him, they haven't tried Him for themselves. You can't know Him and remain the same. When you call Him and mean it, things *change*. I will put my trust in Him today. For the bills, the problems, the test results and anything else. My God lives someplace other than in print or in the imaginations of some ancient pagan historians. Not in history, but in **His** story. "Who we gonna call? JESUS. For a powerful testimony please read 2 Kings 18 and 19. Then Hold On and just believe. Today, is a great day, for a miracle revelation.

SO HOLDON 2 OVERCOME. H2O

Bring a Rope

When the soldiers come for Daniel he doesn't argue or struggle. He had already made up his mind that he would stand and not bow. Daniel was ready to die for His God. He's praying as they usher him out of his house and then suddenly Daniel turns and points towards the corner. He asks the captain of the guard that was sent to retrieve him if he would kindly bring that rope hanging over there in the corner. They hurry him on and in Daniel 6:16 he is brought to the King's court where Daniel is calm and resolved as he faces yet another challenge of his faith this time in the form of hungry, ferocious lions.

He turns and asks that captain, "Did you bring the rope?" They escort Daniel to the lion's den without a battle but on the way Daniel again inquires of that captain guarding him, "Did you remember the rope?" At the mouth of the lion's den with the sound of the roaring in his ears, the smell of death in his nose and the faces of his evil-inspired accusers in his sight he turns and this time orders the captain to, "Get the rope!"

The captain finally gives in to his curiosity and steps towards Daniel to ask, "Why do you keep talking about a rope? I've done this more than a few times and believe you me a rope won't help you in the lion's den."

But unwavering Daniel looks him square in the eyes and replies, "The rope isn't for me, it's for you to use.... because I'm coming back out."

Hold On Family, keep praying and although it may seem like you are heading towards the doom of an inescapable fate, bring your rope. We have to stand today not on what we hear, smell, or see but on the promises of our God. He is still in the miracle working business. He is still making a way out of no way and rescuing His children from harm. Bringing the rope with you is just claiming your victory in advance so with the resolve of Daniel stand firm today. Bring your rope, Today, is a great day, to come back out of the lion's den. So Hold On to it and for it.

HoldOn 2 Overcome. H2O.

My God is Greater

Picture Daniel either sitting or standing with rays of light shining down onto him from above. That is the scene most often depicted in pictures and paintings of Daniel in the Lion's Den. Daniel is calm and the lion's are either laying there peacefully or just walking around disinterested. As warm and fuzzy as that seems, do we really believe it went down that way? Did Daniel really drop in and just casually use a lion as a pillow to sleep peacefully through the night or did those lions snap, growl and roar at him for hours? Did Daniel have the smell of the lion's pit soaked into his garments and were his feet covered with the filth that covered the floor of the den? Was he scratched and scraped if not from lion's claws but from rubbing against the sharp rocks that lined the walls of the cave as he was lowered?

Well folks, I don't know about you but in my personal "Lion's Den" experiences it hasn't been pretty and the lions aren't silent or peaceful. The lion's are doing everything in their power to do what lion's do, seek whom they may devour. So should we be surprised when liars, lie; cheaters, cheat; cancer cripples or poverty depresses? Hold On Family, our God is greater and evil will not prevail. In Daniel 6:22 it says "My God has sent his angel and has shut the lions' mouths." But don't miss the fact that shutting the lion's mouth didn't only stop the lion from devouring Daniel (you and I). Shutting the lion's mouth meant they couldn't make all that noise anymore either. Instead of the nerve-racking roaring these huge beasts are reduced to purring softly and Daniel (you and I) could relax and even rest in the middle of what was meant to be the place of death. Maybe that is what David was talking about in Psalms 23.

So today, just like He did for Daniel, God can say, "HUSH" to the lions in your life. Just Hold On, be still and let them wear themselves out growling and attacking if they want to. Say it out loud if you need to. "Hush Lions, my God is greater and today is a great day, for my miracle."

JUST HOLDON 2 OVERCOME. H2O.

My "Oh Reply" Is Coming

There will be sleepless nights and King Darius had just had one of them. The Bible records in Daniel 6:18 that "his sleep fled from him." I imagine few people in the whole kingdom slept that night, not even Daniel's accusers for they were up celebrating and planning their takeover of Daniel's territory. It's the moment when the haters *think* you are defeated. Throughout the entire kingdom the anticipation was electric. Everyone waited for what would be revealed. As for for King Darius this was a night he would spend in prayer for his friend in the pit of death having been placed there by the King's own misdirected arrogance. The King is offering his loyalty and his life to God in exchange for an answer. That night, King Darius had to Hold On. King Darius gets up at the crack of dawn and runs to the lion's den. It is recorded that the King calls out before he even gets to the pit. He shouts out the first word "Oh." Then he continues with "Servant of the living God, is thy God, whom thou servest continually, able to deliver thee from the lions?" Then Daniel calls back from inside the pit "Oh" and I'll stop right there. Yes, Daniel did shout more words up from that pit of lions that day, but the "Oh" reply was all anyone needed to hear. When they heard that first sound of the first word, "Oh" it was settled right then and the victory was won. "Oh" meant that

Daniel was alive and therefore the prayers had been answered. The "Oh" reply meant that the trial was Oh"ver, Daniel was delivered, God's promises fulfilled and he had "Oh"vercome.

Did you get that Hold On Family, Overcome begins with "Oh" (You can go ahead and shout now) The crowd cheered, the haters cowered in fear and the King said "Get him Oh-U-T of there."

The day is coming when you are going to get to Now repeat after me, "[*say your name*] My Oh Reply is coming. My Oh Reply is coming. Praise, God, my Oh reply is coming!" Today is a great day, for that miracle. Just Hold On.

HoldOn 2 Oh-vercome. H2O

Break Every Chain

Luke 8:29 says "and though he was chained.. he had broken his chains." Mark 5:4 repeats, "For he had often been chained hand and foot, but he tore the chains apart and broke the irons on his feet." No one was strong enough to hold him and even iron shackles didn't stand a chance. Who wouldn't love to have the physical strength to literally break metal chains with only their bare hands? Before admiring this strength let's recognize that the Bible reveals the source of this man's power as demonic possession. The enemy of our souls and his fallen angels can imitate what we think are blessings and prosperity but remember there is always a price to pay.

While it is true that breaking loose from the chains did allow him some mobility and freedom but it did not provide peace. His wrists were still raw and infected where the metal had repeatedly rubbed and irritated his skin. How could he really rest well with the broken chains and large metal cuffs clanking all during the night with every turn? No matter where he went or how he tried to hide them there were always those big metal bands visible for all to see indicating that he was still an escaped prisoner then he met Jesus. Mark 5:15 records that "when they came to Jesus, they saw the man who had been possessed by the legion of demons, sitting there, dressed and in his right mind!" Just like that, no more chains. He was completely free and at peace, clothed and in his right mind.

We can improve, we can educate, elevate and slay. We might be able to loose some burdens but which one of us can take the burdens completely away? Chains and stains, heartaches and pains. Who can heal the wounds, hearts and minds? Who dresses us, erases memories and frees our minds? 2 Corinthians 5:17 tells us that "Therefore if any man be in Christ, he or she is a new creature: old things are passed away (the chains); behold all things are become new (the person)." All it takes is to ask Him. "Father God I thank you. Now please free me and give me peace. In the name of Jesus I pray, Amen."

Can you see him sitting there, still scarred and bruised but his hair is combed, he is shaved, he's wearing clean clothes and he's chuckling as people are telling him about how he used to behave. He's free and ready to go on with a purposeful life and it all began when Jesus broke the chains. Hold On, today is a great day, to let Jesus break your chains.

HOLD ON. HOLDON 2 OVERCOME. H2O

I Won't Complain

In Numbers 21:4 the people became discouraged because the journey was rough. Now verse 5 records, "And the people spake against God and against Moses, wherefore have ye brought us up out of Egypt to die in the wilderness? For there is no bread and there is no water; and our soul loatheth this light bread." Get this. First they said "there is no bread (food), but in the very next breath they say "we don't like this bread."(manna). So which is it? Are they starving or not? And before we get all self-righteous let's be honest and ask ourselves are we guilty of the same complaint? These children of God had stomachs that were filled with food that fell from heaven itself. They had more than they could eat in any one day and blessings did abound. Yet, they are complaining.

Hold On Family, because the beginning of the verse says "the people spake *against* God." That means when we complain about God's blessings (what He sees in His wisdom to supply), we are literally speaking *against* God Himself. Well if that is the case I won't do it. I won't complain any more. God said He's taking me to the promised land. The journey may get rough sometimes but He is keeping me. I do have food (thank you Lord)and I do have water (thank you Lord) and so I won't complain. Sure I can have hopes, big dreams and fancy desires because my Heavenly Father invites me to come boldly and ask Him for anything but He also warns me to not doubt Him by complaining. Instead I'll Hold On and praise Him for the food and water knowing the promised land is near. Just over the horizon and today, is a great day, to feast on milk and honey. Thank you Jesus, I won't complain.

I'LL HOLD ON. HOLDON 2 OVERCOME. H2O

The Death of Death

Yesterday I attended a friend's funeral and today, I miss her. Her life was taken in an accident. Literally she was here one moment and gone the next but my Word promised me that one day "He will wipe every tear from their eyes. There will be no more death or mourning or crying or pain, for the old order of things has passed away."(Revelations 21:4)

Hold On Family and just imagine no more death but not just the usual definition or conditions we might think of, not just decay, disease or divorce but imagine if you can no more subtraction. No more.. less. All life remains and never decreases. No stinky smells of decomposition because food stays fresh forever. No refrigerators, freezers, or preservatives are needed any more. We will never again say "ouch" because our brains will never again register pain because our brains will never again encounter pain. How do I know? Pain won't exist anymore, it's dead. No arguments because all we have is love for each other. We never fall and never fail. We can't get lost. Insurance is unnecessary. Every day is a great day and better than the day before. Just imagine that even on the tiniest cellular level the only thing that exists is life and order. No more mutations means no more cancers. That's why the text says "the old order is passed away." It's going to take a while to get used to this new world with no death. Only breathing fresh air and everything we taste is wonderful. Don't you want to feel it, just life coursing through your body? Walk and never get weary, run and never faint.

Just imagine an eternity of meeting people that you will never have to say goodbye to. We will never miss anybody ever again. After a short while everybody in heaven will be friends and family. Everybody will be a loved one. Hold On for it, the death of death and that great reunion in the sky. If I never see you here, just Hold On. I'll see you in the New Jerusalem.

HoldOn 2 Overcome. H2O. Til then, rest in peace Sue.

Persistent

PER·SIST·ENT

1. REFUSING TO GIVE UP OR LET GO; PERSEVERING OBSTINATELY.

2. EXISTING OR REMAINING IN THE SAME STATE FOR AN INDEFINITELY LONG TIME

For defining words there used to just be one authority, Webster's Dictionary but I think they missed it on this word persistent. The dictionary gives the meaning as, "refusing to give up or let go." Then it goes on with more about *insistence* and *remaining*. Maybe if they referenced the Bible first they would have simply written, "see faith." God, in His holy dictionary gives His definition in Luke 18. The word is introduced in the title "The Parable of the Persistent Widow" and verse 1 gives the definition. "Then Jesus told his disciples a parable to show them that they should *always pray* and *not give up*."

Hold On Family, there it is, the real and true definition from God Himself. They are two separate directives and both are powerful instructions in their own individual right but put them together and we get the answer for any and every challenge we will ever encounter on this chunk of dirt called earth. Now read on in Luke 18 to see what happened for that persistent widow. "The judge ignored her for a while, but eventually she got on his nerves. I fear neither God nor man he said but this woman bothers me. I'm going to see that she gets justice, for she is wearing me out with her constant coming. Then the Lord said, if even an evil judge can be worn down like that, don't you think that God will surely give justice to his people who plead with him day and night? The answer to that question is a definitive and unwavering Yes! He will answer and give justice.

Hold On family, if you are reading this message right now you too can claim that same promise for yourself. Try this affirmation. "If that widow received the justice she sought and if her persistence paid off so will mine." Repeat it with me a few times, "I [*say your name*] will be persistent. I will pray and I will not give up. Pray and not give up." Repeat it, til you mean it and Hold On because today, is a great day, for my miracle.

HoldOn 2 Overcome. H2O

5 Smooth Stones

Why five? "Then he took his staff in his hand, choose five smooth stones from the stream..." (1Samuel 17:40) Why did David pick up five if he knew he would be successful with just one or did he know? David carried two instruments considered weapons. The staff was for close hand-to-hand combat. When it came to challenging this giant he was confident, but not crazy. The sling was for long-range fighting and David was quite proficient with it. I imagine the long hours with the sheep were perfect opportunities for practicing but Goliath was not only large, he was a soldier outfitted in full armor with the latest weaponry for war. This was no ordinary opponent. This was the enemy's champion. (The enemy has his champions in the forms of cancer, addiction, divorce, selfishness etc..) As David approached he sized up this behemoth, determined his optimal target and picked up the ammo in preparation for battle. Hold On Family, when we are drawn into a fight we have to be determined to see it through to victory. No matter what. If the first attempt isn't successful we have to be ready and willing to keep charging, keep swinging and slinging. See, David's confidence and strength was not just in his own ability, might or skills but in his faith to persevere.

God had delivered him from two other killers, the jaws of a lion and the claws of a bear and neither of those were easy. So that day standing there in front of this colossal killer he determined it may take a few throws/tries but he was not giving up. You and I have to be just as determined that we are going to be victorious if we are willing to see it through without giving up. I'm going to keep believing and fighting until I'm standing on the battlefield naked having thrown all the stones, the sling, the staff, my pouch, my sandals and even my tunic at that giant. Do I give up now? No! David nor the rock killed the giant that day.

Our God drops giants! 1 Samuel 17:47 "And all this assembly shall know that the Lord saveth not with sword and spear: for the battle is the Lord's and He *will* give you into our hands." So only one stone was needed for the giant, the other four were for faith and anybody else who needed convincing once Goliath fell. David, standing there with his sling still in his hand was making the ultimate proclamation of faith. "You see what just happened? Anybody else wanna try me? Well, there's more where that came from and today you will know what my Lord can do." Hold On, [*say your name*] the giant is going down! Keep the faith and don't give up because today, is a great day, for my giant to fall.

HOLDON 2 OVERCOME. H2O

Andre the Giant

At 12 this man was already 6'3" and weighed 200 pounds. In this picture he is 7'4" and weighs over 500 pounds. Fact is you can pass a silver dollar through the ring he wore on his pinky finger and your whole hand through the ring for another of his fingers. I remember when I was a kid watching Andre the Giant wrestle and being amazed at his size and strength. Literally, he was unbeatable.

In my own personal struggle with faith I'm drawn to David. So what kind of faith would a 150 pound high school boy wearing a tunic and a pair of sandals have to attack someone the size of Andre the Giant who was wearing a full suit of armor and carrying very large weapons? Not to mention this giant also had an entire army behind him for backup? To come on the scene, see and hear what's going on and then proclaim I'll fight him! Crazy?

Which of us would volunteer to contract cancer just to prove that God will heal us? What David did was the worst example of military strategy in the history of man? He had no protection, no backup plan, no exit strategy, no distractions or cover, no negotiations, no air-strikes or first wave. What kind of faith was that? Just grab what you know, some stones and go charging at this giant man-killer?

David's words from the battlefield that day are recorded in 1 Samuel 17:45 "You come against me with the sword and spear and javelin, but I come against you in the name of the Lord Almighty, the God of the armies of Israel." I declare to you today that no matter what the giant's size or name. Whether you're struggling with illness, unemployment or depression, addiction or divorce you can step up to the challenge confident that you will have the victory. Claim it and know that God will keep His word. That David kind of faith is still available to us today and you too will step up to the giants you may face and proclaim I'll fight him! Pray it and Hold On with me. God said it. I believe it and that settles it.Now in the name of the Lord Almighty, the God of the armies of Israel, you're going down! Today, is a great day, for conquering giants. Just Hold On.

HoldOn 2 Overcome. H2O

Can You believe?

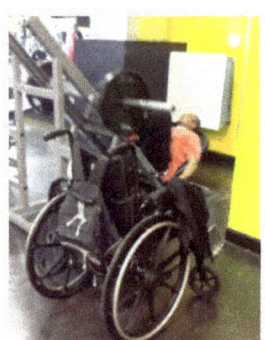

A picture is worth a thousand words. This man came to the gym in a wheelchair. Just let that sink in for a moment. A van pulls up to the entrance and delivered him to the door and from there he was on his own. His first challenge was actually maneuvering up and over a steep curb and then he had to get inside through these heavy swinging doors. He is undaunted. Once inside he wheels himself to an elliptical machine and then hoists himself up and out of the chair and carefully places his unwilling feet onto the footboards. He literally has to use his hands to push his legs to get them moving. After a short "warm up" period he lets himself back down into the chair and wheels over to the apparatus in the picture, the leg press machine. Can you believe this? A man that can barely stand is coming to work out his legs. I introduced myself and helped as much as he would allow me but mostly I just marveled at his determination and felt unworthy for the healthy legs that I have.

Lawrence and I have become good friends and any time I need a little reminder I can just look at this picture. See, Lawrence has decided NOT to accept the diagnosis or prognosis of Multiple Sclerosis. Lawrence has said, "My God is greater." Every time he comes to this gym his presence changes the whole atmosphere in the place. No matter how tired you may be or how tough your day is. No matter what challenges you're facing, what didn't go right this morning, or what prayers have or haven't been answered there is a man in a wheelchair working out so you better move your butt! Everybody has to pick it up a notch, add some weight, do a few more reps. If you weren't sweating before you better get to sweating now.

Lawrence thinks I helped him that day but in actuality he helped me far greater than words can express. Not a single complaint or grumble passed from his lips. No pity parties or excuses did he give. That day I got to be in the presence of a living, walking, talking, leg-pressing witness for faith and determination. Keep this picture if you need a reminder. If Lawrence can keep pressing on and holding on, then so can I.

HOLD ON. HOLDON 2 OVERCOME. H2O

Detour to Destiny

We had left the house which will be named point A to go to point B. After completing the task at point B we left to drive back to point A. Arriving back at Point A we were missing something and could only guess it had been left back at Point B. So we drive back to point B and then back again to point A all the while realizing that all these extra detours and running around will most likely make us late for point C, D and even eventually point E. As we drive back up at point A we encountered a man just walking up the street talking rather loudly on his cell phone and it is quite evident that he is upset because he is yelling and cursing. I exited my car and called out to get his attention. I started by speaking to him calmly and nicely asked him if he would mind not using the profanity so loudly in the presence of the children and myself. Apparently he didn't think a vocabulary change was necessary and he turns in my direction, crossed the street and proceeded to come close enough to me to be considered a threat. I'm not afraid but not stupid either so I take a defensive stance. He gets so close that I hear him mumble under his breath that no one cares. Standing there I looked deep into this young man's eyes and I recognized pain, confusion, distrust and a few other things.

I determined at that moment to try to make a difference in his life and knew that I had a good chance because he wouldn't expect it. I responded with the intention of speaking to his very soul, "Yes someone does care. I care and God cares because He sent me right here at this exact time just for you." He stopped right there in his tracks and stared at me with a bewildered look on his face. While he gazed at me apparently trying to process the beyond-happenstance depth of this moment I recapped the morning's shenanigans and all the miles between points A and B that I had traveled to end up right here in front of him at the perfect moment. I could tell that he got it. He knew *it was no accident* that I was standing there, right then at that precise moment to speak to him.

Neither one of us had any idea or plans to meet each other that morning, yet here we stood. We had both experienced a detour to destiny. We eventually prayed together and needless to say became acquaintances and talked many times after that day. He said I changed his life that day but that's not actually correct. He gave me purpose. It was just a detour with a purpose.

Proverbs 3:5.6 says "… and lean not on your own understanding. In all your ways submit to Him and He *will* direct your paths." Hold On, there are and will always be delays, reschedules, unforeseen obstacles and postponements but there just may be more going on from the realms of heaven than what meets our eyes here on earth. God *is* in control and He's aligning paths so that we can be assured and declare all things are working for me, for my good and for His glory! In the meantime, look for the reasons and the purpose for why you are where you are at any given moment. Today, is a great day, to discover a detour to your destiny.

HoldOn 2 Overcome. H2O.

Rest Stop

You've been planning to take a vacation and now you are on the road driving south to Florida. White sand beaches, palm trees and warm salty breezes await your arrival. It isn't long before you see the first sign at the side of the road that says "Rest Stop Ahead." The closer you get to the actual area to pull off there are more and more rest stop signs. If you've ever taken a road trip you know that the journey can include a few quick stops or a lot of long and wearisome stops that can add hours to the original ETA. Inevitably a stop is necessary and so you take an exit and follow the signs to park at the rest stop. Remarkably you find that the landscaping is beautiful. The vending machines are all stocked with chips, soda's and even some healthy choices. There are pristine and sparkling toilets sitting neatly in unmarred stalls and it even smells....pleasant. There's a playground out back for the kids and plenty of friendly engaging new friends to converse with. This place is so nice maybe we will decide to just stay right here instead of trekking hundreds of miles further South. We can camp here in the car and survive by eating junk food. I bet you are shaking your head right now at the ridiculousness of the concept. Trade the beauty of palm trees, white sand and beach sunsets for a roadside pitstop? Who would do such a ridiculous thing?

Let's read John 14:2-3. "In my Father's house are many mansions: if it were not so, I would have told you. I go to prepare a place for you. And if I go and prepare a place for you, I will come again and receive you unto myself; that where I am, there ye may be also." Hold On Family, I propose to you today that no matter how good things may seem, how nice your home is, how satisfying your education or career are, how obedient your children, how respected your friends are or how high your bank account or credit score, no matter how much success you may be experiencing, you are only at a rest stop and this place is not our home nor the final destination. Believers, what happened to the message of Jesus is coming again so get ready?

All these prosperity messages, preachers, teachers, coaches and churches are all trying to sell us on the rest stop. The message repeated in His word is that there is something far greater, better and sweeter. In John 14:3 Jesus Himself tells us, "I go to prepare a place for you….I will come back and get you…so you can be there with me." And 1 Corinthians 2:9 says "No eyes have ever seen, nor ears heard, neither has anyone even imagined the things God has prepared for those that love Him." He said He's coming back to get us and take us away from this contaminated stuff on this earth but He loves us so much that He still gives us a choice. If you love it here so much, He will let you stay but you're probably not going to like what's going to happen.

Just answer this one question, "Why did Jesus have to go through all of that and die on the cross, to let me have the things of this world?" The answer is He didn't. He died so that we could go there, not stay here. This place needs a total makeover and He has a plan to remake it even better than the original but first, He's going to take us to the beach beside the sea of glass.

No rest stop living for me, no sir. I want to go all the way to the final destination. No more pain or sorrows, together forever with everyone I love. How about you? Well Hold On then because today, is a great day, to resume your journey to the promised land. Let's Hold On together.

Just HoldOn 2 Overcome. H2O

Auto On

Before getting into the shower I placed my Samsung smartphone on the nearby sink basin in the bathroom. I turned on the hot water and got into what has become a chapel of sorts for talks with God. A private place where the warmth of the water hugs you, the pounding droplets relax you and little streams of water running down your face don't mean that you're crying or weak. I was in there praying from the bottom of my soul then I heard a voice close by and definitely *in* the bathroom with me. A scene straight from a movie. I peered from my steamy retreat to see that my cell phone screen was illuminated. It was on. Yes, it had automatically, all by myself, untouched by human hands just turned itself on and had even bypassed the password. It then navigated itself to the Tunein Radio app, chose WJOU 90.1 out of my favorites and began playing that station. I pulled the curtain back further in disbelief just in time to hear a song end and then the lady DJ came on and said these exact words,"Our text for today is Romans 16:20. "The God of peace will soon crush Satan under your feet. The grace of our Lord Jesus be with you." That was all she said. Another song started playing and I just stood there stunned out of my mind. How could this happen? What I had just experienced is technologically impossible. Phones just don't come on.

But Hold On Family, I was praying. When the odds seem hopeless and humanly impossible. When even the physical body has begun to break under the strain. When the enemy is trying to break our spirits, block our blessings and keep us from the destiny we are called to and promised. God will do something, send a message, a burning bush, a pillar of fire, or maybe He'll turn on a phone to remind us to trust and don't give up. I believe that message was no accident. It was a promise from the Word, that was with God, is God and can not fail. It was a message for me that day and it is a message for you right now. I suggest you read it and then write that verse down. Repeat it in faith and believe soon God will crush satan under my feet! Just keep Holding On.

HoldOn 2 Overcome. H2O

Shanghaied

A senior African American gentleman relayed this story to me. The year was 1954 and he was just a teenager living in rural South Carolina. One evening he borrowed his brother's car to travel to where he worked at the Fort Jackson Army base located in Columbia, SC. He was driving and there were 3 other service men in the car as passengers. The group just happened to drive past the local sheriff, a Caucasian man, who saw them and turned his car around to follow them and then pulled them over. The sheriff released the soldiers and let them walk to the nearby base, but not my friend who is relaying this story to me today. He said considering the racial tension at that time he was quite relieved when the sheriff eventually let him go also. Then, two weeks later my friend receives a letter delivered in his name. He was ordered to report for army duty at Ft. Jackson but he had never enlisted, signed any papers, or even expressed an interest in joining the armed forces. He told me that the letter reported that they had even waived the necessary physical exam and he had already been officially accepted to serve. He then found out that the sheriff who had detained him and took his driver's license a couple weeks ago had also signed him up for the army.

My friend had literally been "Shanghaied." So due to fear of repercussions from that unscrupulous sheriff and/or the army, he reported for duty, completed the training and was then shipped off to serve in a war. While I'm standing there with my mouth and eyes open wide in utter amazement he then says, "It's the best thing that happened to me at that time."

Jeremiah 29:11 says "For I know the plans I have for you," declares the Lord, "plans to prosper you and not to harm you, plans to give you hope and a future." Hold On Family, I relay this story to remind you, to strengthen you, to reassure us all that our God is in control. No matter how it looks, seems, feels, or appears, He controls today and tomorrow. So we are never Shanghaied, only guided by His all-powerful hand. Repeat this with me. "I am determined to see it through. To know just what the Lord will do."

My friend served honorably, was discharged and went on to a long, prosperous life and career. He's 91 years old today and I usually see him at the gym still working out. Hold On Family, our God promised that He would work it all out for our good even if we are shanghaied. He promised, so see it through.

HOLD ON. HOLDON 2 OVERCOME. H20.

The Tearless

The soul would have no rainbow if the eyes had no tears.
Native American proverb

What a sight it will be to see heaven. Imagine with your wildest possible imaginations the joy and wondrousness of it all. Besides the singing, shouts of triumph, reunions with loved ones, meeting the angels and no more aches and pains there will be those streets of gold and a sea of glass and we'll finally meet Jesus. Even with all those people celebrating and amongst all the throngs of angels there will be a little section that is empty with a banner hanging above that reads "The Tearless." A few of the saints inquire and Jesus reports that He had still reserved a space for those that had chosen to lead carefree lives without sacrifices, struggles or trials. He had offered the same promises and His life as a sacrifice for the wealthy, the stars and people of status and renown. So that no one would be left out He solicited the dignitaries and tried to save all the rich young rulers but sadly none of those people made it. They just didn't want to come. They just didn't see a need for all that faith and religion stuff and instead they chose to hold on to their lives, their jobs, their entertainments, their comforts and their own gods. There is a moment of silence in heaven as the new inhabitants gaze around at their surroundings and shake their heads at the wonder that someone actually chose not to see glory and all that had been prepared for them. Jesus solemnly takes the banner down and then there's a loud joyous shout as the saints forget their earthly cares to return to the wondrous scenes before them.

Jesus turns and says, "Welcome one and all. In my Father's house are many mansions: if it were not so, I would have told you. I go to prepare a place for you. And if I go and prepare a place for you, I will come again and receive you unto myself; that where I am, there ye may be also."(John 14:2-3) Heaven is filled with shouts of praise as throngs of joyous, bright angels take flight in uncontained and overwhelming jubilation. Hold On Family, Hold On. He keeps His promises. There is a reward for my labor and I [*say your name*] am going to see it all on that great day. The tears today will be traded for joy everlasting.

So Hold On for it. HoldOn 2 Overcome. H2O

Time

$\mathcal{D}$o you ever just want to ask God why is it taking sooo long for the breakthrough, the turnaround, the harvest or the healing? Time can be a deal breaker. Well consider this. God in His wisdom knows that if you knew how long it was going to take, you wouldn't do it. If God said six days, you'd say "thank you Lord." If He said six weeks, you might say "Ok Lord." If God said six months how many would waver, shake their head and look for an easier way out? What if God said six years? Does the thought of years usher in doubt and despair? Forget it Lord. How many people never officially say that but many have loosened their grip on faith with the passing of time?

By applying grace and mercy God breaks it up for us into little pieces that we can handle. He balances the hills and valleys with spaces in between. His design even separated the day from the night to allow us to rest from our battles and then awaken each morning to a new day, a new chance, another opportunity to be victorious. I don't know how much longer this trial will last but I know who does know. (Mercy Jesus). No matter how long it may be I just have to be determined to Hold On. Lamentations 3:21-25, 31- 33, "Yet this I call to mind and therefore I have hope: Because of the Lord 's great love we are not consumed, for his compassions never fail. They are new every morning. Great is your faithfulness!" I'm giving thanks for this day, this hour, this moment in time that I can Hold On knowing who holds even time in His hands. Time after time claim the promises and just keep praying. "Joy cometh in the morning," and it won't be long. Today, brought you closer to the breakthrough.

HoldOn 2 Overcome. H2O

Super Bloom

I heard the radio describe it as a "Super Bloom." The story is about the place aptly named Death Valley, California which is known for being the driest place in the entire U.S. of A and the hottest place on earth. Surely hot and dry is not the optimal environment for flowers to bloom and flourish yet the story is about thousands upon thousands of wildflowers that are covering the ground where only snakes and lizards usually dare to survive. Where there was only sand as far as the eyes can see, now there is instead a vast desert covered in color. Now Hold On for the reason because it is a great message of encouragement for all of us today. See, there had been a drought in this area for a long time, (the dry spells in our lives when we just can't seem to go forward) but then there was a long steady rain throughout the winter (that breakthrough I have been praying for) which soaked down deep into the parched earth and touched seeds that had been deposited there previously in some unknown fashion, left alone ungerminated and surely forgotten for who knows how long (the promise I found and have claimed from His word). When God declares that the timing is right He then shifts the atmosphere (the warmth of the Son)and LIFE is born into what has been patiently waiting. One authority on botany and all things plant life stated that some of these little seeds had probably been buried for decades, maybe a century or *more*. He explained that some of these areas hadn't seen water in 10, 15, or 20 years and now they are a blanket of flowers. In other words, they are survivors! Did you catch that? Survivors.

Here a park ranger maybe unbeknownst to himself is preaching a Hold On sermon of epic proportions. You may just have to go back and read that again and then take a few moments to just let it sink in as to the magnitude of the message. The flowers in bloom today, which were buried in the worst hopeless conditions on earth yesterday, are now sitting in full bountiful and beautiful bloom, *Survivors*. Next to the cactus that usually soaks up all the moisture that the seeds could possibly have used are all these little flowers, *Survivors*. Now people are coming from near and far, literally from all over the world to see not the cactus but the flowers, the *Survivors*. Psalms 19:1 "The heavens declare the glory of God; and the firmament showeth his handy work."

Today the desert declares God's handiwork in a glorious display of new life that waited for the breakthrough. Psalms 2:14 instructs us to "wait on the Lord: be of good courage. And He shall strengthen our hearts. Wait I say on the Lord." I propose that today, is a great day, for God to declare His handiwork in the life of [*Say your name*] also. Yes Lord. I am a *Survivor*. Where there was only desert sand, there will be flowers. I will have my SUPERBLOOM." That's right. Hold On and keep praying.

HOLD ON. HOLDON 2 OVERCOME. H2O

Troubled

In Daniel 2:2 the Bible uses the term troubled. Verse 12 says "For this cause the king was angry and very furious and commanded to destroy all the wise men of Babylon." The king is bewildered, frustrated, out of options and at his wits end. He is the ruling monarch and yet everything he can think of and possibly think to do just won't work this time. Everyone he's called on has failed him. This dream thing is important and it won't let him rest and since he can't remember he doesn't even know what to ask or pray for. There is no way out and so he's *troubled*. Have you ever been there, not even knowing how to pray or what to pray for? Through a turn of divine events Daniel is called in, he prays about the situation and God reveals the king's dream to him. Daniel goes into the King's court and tells it all. Now in verse 46-47, the king who is finally relieved from the distress and overjoyed with the answers jumps off his throne, falls to his knees with his face to the ground and declares, "Of a truth it is, that Your God is a God of Gods and a Lord of Kings."

Hold On Family, therein lies the answer to our dilemmas, struggles and troubling situations as well. God is arranging it all so there will be *no* doubt. The magicians couldn't do it then and your job can't do it now. The wise men couldn't do it then and the bottle of booze can't do it now. His advisors couldn't do it then and your friends can't do it now. The king couldn't do it then and I [*say your name*] can't do it now. Only Jesus can! You can work and work some more. You can try and lie, fake and take, then deny and cry but it still won't fix it. Go to church to shout, cast it out, grin and sin but you will still be *troubled* until you drop to those knees and declare like King Darius "You are the God of Gods and Lord of Lords. Jesus, I believe. Now please take away this trouble." That's all you have to do. Now Hold On, because today, is a great day, to be set free from your troubles.

JUST HOLDON 2 OVERCOME. H2O

Believe and Start Home

In John 4:46 we find Jesus traveling back to Galilee the location of his first public miracle. It was at Galilee that Jesus became an instant celebrity by turning plain old water into the best tasting non-GMO, organic, no preservatives or artificial sweeteners added grape juice ever tasted. There is a man that the word refers to as a nobleman living in the area and he has a son that is suffering from a life-threatening disease. When the loving father hears that this same miracle-working Jesus is back in town he quickly begins to search for him in hopes that maybe, just maybe, Jesus could work another of the miracles he had been hearing about in the form of a healing for His son. Maybe this father had personally witnessed a Jesus miracle or maybe he tasted some of that Jesus Juice himself. Whatever the case the dad finds Jesus and asks for His help without waiver but what really stood out while reading this passage was verse 50,"Jesus said to him, "Go your way; your son lives." So the man believed the word that Jesus spoke to him and he went his way." The NIV translation says "the man took Jesus at his word and departed." The Amplified version puts it like this, "And the man put his trust in what Jesus said and started home." After Jesus said those words the father didn't ask, "are you sure?"

Hold On Family, to exercise Nobleman Faith we have to go

our way. We have to believe that Jesus can make it happen. Be willing to seek Him out. Ask Him and then depart believing it has happened already. (Help us Jesus.) We have to start home, walking, riding, crawling, just start home. That nobleman father went hoping and believing to find Jesus but he returned from his meeting with Jesus knowing and testifying of His power that heals even from a distance. Faith is a verb which means it is an *action* word. You can read the rest of John 4 to see what happens but in the meantime believe and start home. Take a moment and say it now, "I [*say your name*] am going to ask, believe and start home." Then there's nothing else to do but Hold On for it.

HOLDON 2 OVERCOME. H2O.

Current Condition

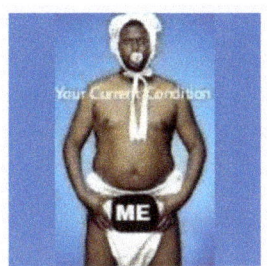

*I*magine a friend is seeking employment and asks you for help with their resume. They come to your house as agreed. You answer the door and your friend is standing there wearing a big, dirty, diaper. What would you think? What do you say? Where do you even begin? "OK, I know you asked for help with your resume but first I have a question. Do you realize that you're wearing a diaper? Why? We have a LOT of work to do here before we even get to the resume part."

Wait a minute reader before you get all self-righteous again, just imagine how we look to God? Coming to Him for help with our lists and pleadings to get what we want just like big spoiled babies that are wearing diapers. Isaiah 64:6 says, "But we are all as an unclean thing and all our righteousness are as filthy rags; and we all do fade as a leaf; and our iniquities, like the wind, have taken us away." Hold On Family, at one time or another we have all looked ridiculous. Before God can even help us with our wish lists first He has to deal with our current condition. It's apparent that we can't see ourselves and the true depth of our utter messed-up-ed-ness. We come to God with what we think are best intentions and convictions but it's actually just amazing that He even allows us into His presence at all with our filthy rags and unpleasant aroma.

God is willing and able to help us but first we have to acknowledge and allow Him to remove the diapers. We have to be willing to give it to Him and accept His will. To make progress we will have to relinquish the messes that we have begun to accept and in many cases cherish. Isaiah 64:8 says "But now, O LORD, You are our Father; We are the clay and You our potter; And all we are the work of Your hand." Hold On, He's reshaping you. Hold On, he's healing the wounds, preparing the place and reprogramming your hard drive. He's fixing you so there will be no more need for diapers. It may take a little while, some struggles and trials, but a favorite song by the Hawkins Singers says "The potter wants to put you back together again." Yes Lord, clean us up, put us back together and give us strength to endure I pray." Now, Hold On. Today, is a great day, for a change in your condition.

So HoldOn 2 Overcome. H2O

Fall In Place

$\mathcal{A}$fter a lengthy period of trying and a hard push for a deadline, things just didn't pan out the way it would have, could have, should have. Have you ever been there, working and waiting, hoping and praying? Well that's just where I was this particular day when I walked through this doorway. I had my keys in my hand when the key fob fell to the ground causing the plastic casing to come apart. As my luck would have it, that little battery that powers the fob fell directly, squarely, right smack dab into this little hole on the ground. Impossible? Incredible. If I would have stood above that same hole and dropped that same battery ten thousand times I bet it would never fall right in that hole like it just did. If my life depended on it I could never get that little battery in that hole. So while I'm still standing there shaking my head and contemplating this battery bullseye that voice that speaks to the back of my mind just said, "Hold On! At the precise right moment it's all going to fall in place just like that battery. Incredibly, inexplicably, just fall in place."

Hold On Family, we just have to keep going. How many words or phrases are there for giving up? Well there's bend, quit, fold, surrender, settle, throw in the towel, wave the white flag, compromise, hide, turn around, end it all just to name a few. Whatever the phrase, don't do that, Hold On instead. No matter how bad you may want to stay in the bed with the covers pulled over your head, get up! Just take a look at that picture and try to imagine the odds of that battery falling into a hole just barely bigger than itself. It did fall in place and so will whatever it is you are praying about. Just take a closer look at the picture and repeat these words. "It will fall in place for me. I don't have to understand it, I just have to wait for it. It will fall in place for me." I know you're tired, Hold On. I know it's heavy and you did your best, Hold On. You are correct that it's not fair, Hold On. No one knows, understands, or cares, Hold On. Read with me Habakuk. 2:3 "For the revelation awaits an appointed time; it speaks of the end and will not prove false. Though it linger, wait for it; it will certainly come and will not delay." That's a promise, in, of and from the Creator Himself. Read it, claim it, repeat it to God as His own Word. His own promise that can not fail. Yes Lord, today is a great day for my miracle. All I have to do is Hold On until it falls into place.

HoldOn 2 Overcome. H2O

Fear or Faith

Sometimes we have to have those not-so-pretty conversations with God where we ask the tough questions like How can I be joyous in my sorrow? Lord, you want me to count it all joy and rejoice and be exceeding glad? Glad God, really? You want me to be happy about this? How can I be glad? Don't you see what I'm going through here God? Lies and attacks. Pain, sickness, suffering and tears. I do believe that you can fix it Lord. I do have faith in you Lord but can you really expect me to be OK with all that is going on right now? Sometimes while we are still praying, Jesus answers, "Well, give it to me then. All of it. You're still holding on to...Fear."

Hold On Family, fear is that thing you keep thinking about. The thing you keep asking but what if? Fear is the very thing that the devil tries to keep you focused on and won't let you have peace about? It creeps into your thoughts and dreams. People unknowingly bring up that subject or ask you a question about it. Songs come on the radio or shows on the TV that remind you of your fears. Everywhere you turn you are tormented with this trepidation and fear. So we often try to rationalize by thinking "if God loves me and hears me, He wouldn't let this happen to me. Maybe He doesn't hear, won't answer, doesn't exist?"

We know that God can work miracles because we have all kinds of evidence from His Word and we hear the testimonies of so many others that appear to be doing well. But even with the positive examples right in front of us there is that fear that is blocking our faith and since it hasn't happened for us yet we question God's ability and willingness to do it for *me*. The enemy wants to make fear personal. He can't stop blessings from occurring so he will actually put the successes of others right in front of you to taunt you. Someone else gets the promotion you've been working towards. Someone else takes the trip and purchases the car you always dreamed of. The enemy tries to get you to think that it's only you so that you will fear the windows of heaven have shut. Well, what you're practicing is doubt and doubt questions God's power and His promises. The fact is, fear and faith cannot coexist.

Hold On Family, try this for a visual. Faith is not standing beside the water. Faith is not clutching the ladder in the shallows of the kiddie pool. No, faith is running towards the deep end of a pool full of hungry sharks and shouting "JESUS" as you cannonball into the middle of the man eaters. Daniel 3 is faith *in* the fiery furnace. Daniel 6 is faith *in* the lion's den and today is a great day to start practicing defeating the fear by exercising the faith. Let's look at Mark 5:36 "Overhearing what they said, Jesus told him, "Don't be afraid; just believe." Luke 8:50 says "Hearing this, Jesus said to Jairus, "Don't be afraid; just believe and she will be healed." It's just a fact that this tug-o-war with fear is just the enemy trying to block your blessings. No matter who gets or does what. No matter how long you've been praying and how long it's taking you have got to practice believing it will over worrying what's going to happen if it doesn't. So start right now by asking God to take away fear and strengthen faith. Hold On, because today, is a great day, to trade fear for faith.

HoldOn 2 Overcome. H2O

CSI

    dvances in technology have meant advances in crime-solving as well. The show's title CSI stands for Crime Scene Investigation. On these shows they use detailed oriented professionals, ground-breaking technology and the evidence found at crime scenes to solve some difficult cases. Techno-cops using advances such as infrared imaging from satellites, facial recognition programs and DNA usually capture the culprit.

    But Hold On Family, believe it or not there is another investigative show that's airing locally and around the world right now. You don't need cable or any special equipment to see it. Every single second and detail is collected, identified and entered into evidence. This case will be solved because of CSI; "Christ Sees It." Psalms 10:14 "But you GOD, see the trouble of the afflicted; you consider their grief and take it in hand. The victims commit themselves to you; you are the helper of the fatherless."

    That's right, Christ sees us here but praise God that's not all the verse says. It also says that "to those who commit themselves to Him, he helps them." God is telling you to give it to Him and let Him help you. If you need to just say it or pray it out loud feel free to do so. CSI. Christ Sees It. Christ sees [*say your name*].

The job, the family, the doctor's report, CSI. The pain, the car, the scandal, CSI. The courtroom, the friends, the church, the house, CSI. Christ sees it all and Christ always solves the case. So Hold On and keep going because the evidence is mounting that today, is a great day, for your miracle. As they say on the show "the evidence never lies."

So Hold On 2 Overcome. H2O

Willing, Able and Ready

*A*re you W.A.R.? Are you Willing, Able and Ready? *Willing* means you have shaken off the chains of self, me and my. You have escaped from the selfishness of I want, I think and I need. Willing is simply "what do You have for me Lord? I'm ready to follow." Then the next part *Able* means can I go when the call comes? Do I have the ability to act? Is there something or anything at all standing in the way? Anything that would keep me from walking into my destiny? Is there anyone that I may not be able to walk away from? Am I physically able to get up and follow? Then there is *Ready* which means today, right now, at this very moment you are available and prepared to act on His direction?

Let's be honest here, at this very moment if the phone rang or there was a knock on the door with an invitation to pursue what you've been waiting for, could you go? Ask yourself, have I prepared for this breakthrough moment or have I been just talking about it? Now think of the heroes, the prophets, the leaders that you read about in the Word and consider some that may have been *willing* but not ready, *ready* but not *able*. There are many combinations but today I propose that if you really want to know… If you really want a definitive answer… If you *really* want to receive an answer from the Lord, pray this prayer.

"Father God, thank you for another day of possibility. Now please help me to be Willing, Able and Ready. I claim your promises and offer myself at this very moment to be your instrument and to be used for your glory. Please reveal my purpose and your will for my life in a way so profound that I will know that it is the answer I have prayed for. In Jesus' name, Amen."

Matthew 9:9 reads "Jesus said to Matthew follow me. And he arose and followed Him." Take a moment and think of the others that had their lives forever changed in one moment of one day. Prepare for W.A.R. Be *Willing* to answer the call. *Able* if the call came today and *Ready* because today is a great day for my revelation and breakthrough. You've prayed for it, so now all you have to do is look for it and Hold On.

HoldOn 2 Overcome. H2O.

Supreme Package Deal

Unless we are very wealthy we all like to stretch our resources. Most of us make an effort to get the most out of every dollar and so we look for the discounts: the BOGO, the bundle, the warehouse stores for bulk buys, the package deal. Who wouldn't want to apply the same principle to blessings? Wouldn't we love to get several answers with one prayer? Wouldn't it be great to have a BOGO coupon or get a package deal promotion when approaching God's throne with our requests?

Well imagine the number of things that were on Joseph's prayer request list that pivotal morning he last woke behind bars. In Genesis. 41:8 we find Joseph surely praying about a laundry list of things. Could we imagine he was praying about his freedom, food, clothing, temperature control, separation anxiety, anger management, loneliness, unsatisfactory living conditions and unfulfilled promises just to name a few? Some of the things he may have been praying about then are some of the same things that we may be praying about now. On this particular morning while Joseph is still imprisoned in the dungeon he is summoned. Just a little while later he is shaved, dressed in new clothes and standing in all places before the King. The King conveys a riddle in the form of a dream and Joseph prayed for the answer. Joesph receives the answer from God and gives credit to God for conveying the meaning of the dream to the troubled king. Then in one moment, in the twinkling of an eye, everything changed! It's right there in verse 40 that the King said "Joseph is in charge of...everything."

Hold On Family, it was a package deal. God fixed it *all* and at one time. From prison to palace all in maybe an hour. Hallelujah! A few hours later Joseph is lying in a royal bed, free, fed and warm and verse 45 says married. (Don't give up. Don't settle. Don't stop praying for that Godly mate.) Why do I Hold On? I like Joseph, know what my God is capable of. It's not a prosperity message of wealth and grandeur, it's a message of hope that our situations, problems, sicknesses or failures... whatever it may be, can all be bundled up and turned around in a moment. Any moment. God has a supreme package deal for me [say your name]. There's no expiration date on the offer and the customer service department never closes. So Hold On, Hold On, Hold On. Today, is a great day, for my package deal.

HOLDON 2 OVERCOME. H2O

Victory Over Giants

Have you ever wondered why the King would allow David, whom he said is just a youth, to represent the entire nation of Israel against the giant Goliath? If David loses, they all lose. The King was named Saul and King Saul knew personally what God could and would do for someone who believes in Him. See back in 1 Samuel 10:10 it is recorded that "the spirit of God came upon Saul," then again in chapter 11:6-11 "and with power Saul gained victory over the enemy." Because of his great triumphs as a God-filled man Saul is then made King and rules for 42 years but then Saul in Chapter 15 rebels, disobeys God and in chapter 16:14 it is recorded that the Lord's spirit has *left* Saul. Read one verse before and the Word says Samuel anointed David and the spirit of the LORD "came upon" David and stayed with him. This spirit on David was able to cast away the evil spirit on King Saul when it tormented him. Saul was familiar with spirits and he recognized and knew that the Lord was with David. Saul believed the account of David conquering a bear and a lion with his bare hands. So now in chapter 17:37 when David says "The Lord that delivered me out of the paw of the lion and out of the paw of the bear, he will deliver me out of the hand of this Philistine," Saul believes it because he knew how possible the impossible is when God's Spirit is on a man. So the once God-filled King Saul puts the fate of his whole nation in the hands of this teenage shepherd boy by commanding, "Go and the Lord be with thee."

Hold On Family, King Saul didn't have faith in David. He had faith in God! King Saul knew full well what can happen when the Lord is with you and I declare that today the same still holds true and that's a mighty great reason to shout. For Romans 8:31 forever reminds us that "If God be for us, who can stand against us?" Hold On, for the Spirit that is with us has already won the battle. Down goes our giants and any other attack from the enemy. *"Lord, thank you. Now please let your Spirit fall on me and I will give you all the praise and glory for the victory. Amen."* Now Hold On because today, is a great day, for that victory.

HoldOn 2 Overcome. H2O

It's Only Temporary

In God's Word Jesus clearly speaks of life and death. He specifically lays out His plan for returning to get those who chose Him as their Savior. It is recorded for us in 2 Thessalonians 4:17 that those that were born and then went to sleep in death will be the first one's that will rise up in the air to meet Jesus when he returns to earth, just as He promised He would do in John 14:1-3. There will be some people who walk this earth that will never die at all. The righteous men and women still alive walking on the earth who chose to obey and claim the gift of salvation through Jesus Christ will be caught up in the air to meet Him and they will never experience the sleep of death. (2 Thessalonians 4:17). Lazarus is one of those who will have experienced death at least twice. He was born, went to sleep (John 11:14) with a sickness, was raised from the dead by Jesus (John 11:43, 12:1,9,17), but then he eventually went to sleep in death again to await the second coming.

Jesus Himself said in John 11:4 "this sickness is not unto death...." The NIV says "This sickness will not END in death." Hold On Family, what jumped off the page at me is that this situation I may be facing, similar to the sickness Lazarus was facing, is *not* unto death meaning permanent. Let's personalize it by repeating this fact. My [say your name] current situation, dilemma, or whatever it is I'm facing it is *not* permanent. It's only temporary. The story will not end this way and there is more to come. How do we know? Because Jesus said it. So take heart and pray for the resurrection of your situation. Is the bank account empty? Is the car battery dead, the tires bald and the gas gauge on empty? Are there notices from the bill collectors and the utilities shut off? Are the kids out of control and the loneliness unbearable? Are you discouraged, depressed and barely holding on? Well read John 11:4 once again and claim it today that my hopeless situation is not unto death. Then move down and read John 11:43 which tells us, "At Jesus' word, Lazarus came forth." Yes, Lazarus came forth and so will I. Now, just keep praying and Holding On.

HoldOn 2 Overcome. H2O.

Sometimes You Have to Deal with the Dogs

*A*s a youngster we lived in the country at the crest of a gently sloping hill. There were no sidewalks or street lights, just miles of two-laned pavement divided by double yellow lines stretching east and west for miles past homes and cornfields. Across the road lived Mr Hall with his four large German Shepherds who loved to terrorize anyone that dared cross into their territory. In the time before video games riding your bike was the method of transportation so after chores and homework I loved to ride to a friend's house. Near or far didn't really matter because the real challenge was always, getting past those dogs. I never quite figured out how they would know but every single time I came out on my bike they would gather at the road preparing to give chase. With wolf-like fangs and demonic snarling, they would run along beside me literally nipping at my heels. Each bicycle venture beyond the driveway required a mental preparation and physical commitment. Even if I made it safely past the hounds from hell leaving I knew they would always be waiting for me on the return trip for yet another round of snapping and pedaling for my life.

Yes these dogs were a big problem and they had plenty of

free time to terrorize anyone that dared pedal by. Recently I have found myself thinking about those dogs pretty often. After decades of not being interested in bicycles I was reintroduced to what is called cycling and I am hooked. It is great exercise. There is a world-wide cycling community to share the passion with and it is probably the most intense sport I have participated in. So on those 40+ mile rides when I'm in the zone giving it all I got to keep pace with a group moving at over 20mph, I think of those dogs that used to chase me and I pedal a little harder.

Those dogs were a great nuisance *but* they taught me some lessons about motivation and determination. Motivation is wanting something, Determination is about how bad you want something. Motivation gets you going, determination keeps you going. Motivation takes you out but it's determination that has to bring you back home again. To ride my bike to a friend's house I had to be both motivated and determined. Hold On Family, it's just a fact of life. Sometimes to get where we want to go, we have to deal with the dogs and just like me on that open road, sometimes we have to go it alone. Nobody else was there to ride with me and even if there were, few people wanted to ride past those German Shepherds. Lastly but still worth focusing on is the fact that dealing with the dogs made me faster. That's right. I learned way back then how to pedal my heart out, ignore the pain and focus on the finish. I knew back then that it was about 100 pedal strokes to be in the clear from those dogs and today I make it up steep inclines by counting pedal strokes to the top. Hills can be conquered one stroke at a time.

Do you know who else was motivated and determined? Jesus. He loved us and wanted to be with us and that was His motivation. So much so that He developed a plan that would satisfy the order that He is and justify His true character to everything He had ever created. In order to prove that lucifer was the liar and make it possible for all disobedience to be washed from the sin-stained human race Jesus decided to pay our debt and take our punishment for us. He showed us the ultimate determination and proved how much He really did love us, enough to come down here to deal with the dogs, to do it alone and He claimed the victory by conquering a hill called Calvary!

I will never know if you read the 100 messages before this one or if you just happened to start at the back of this book and read this one first. Maybe you never ever saw the book and someone sent you this one message or maybe you were picking up some paper on the ground and found this message printed on it. Sometimes God just works like that. Whatever the case I want you to know that beyond a shadow of a doubt it is no accident that you are reading this now. You are the One. You are the reason that I had to Hold On through the decade of trials and tribulations to gather these messages and finally get them into print. You are the One that made it all worthwhile and you are the One He gave His life for and I know you know it's true, because you are reading this right now at this pivotal point in your life.

[*Say your name*] Jesus did it for me and today, is a great day, to accept the gift and overcome.

HOLDON 2 OVERCOME. H2O.

Afterword

The end of these pages is not the end of this journey. As long as there's need to Hold On there will be more Hold On messages. Until that time you can always go to holdon2overcome.com for more inspiration as we make continuous updates.

Also by W. Patrick Harris

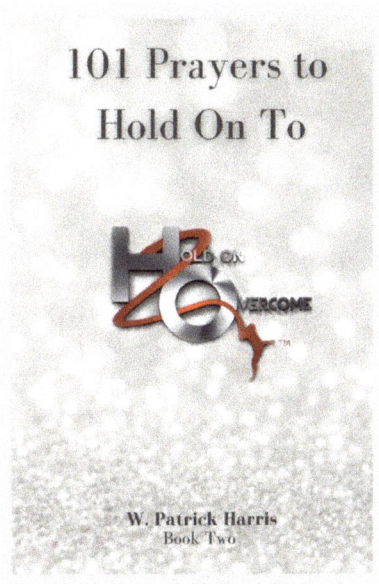

The messages recorded here are actual prayers. They are conversations with God, while sitting at a computer keyboard. They are struggles and pleadings that were typed out on a screen. They were transposed onto paper so that they could be shared with anyone and for as long as people still read. They have been and hopefully will continue to be shared for as long as people need to speak with God. Until He returns and we can all speak to Him face to face. Pray On. Pray On to Overcome.

www.ingramcontent.com/pod-product-compliance
Lightning Source LLC
Chambersburg PA
CBHW062021290426
44108CB00024B/2735